Gran Bretagna

Tables Requisite to be Used with the Astronomical and Nautical Ephemeris

Gran Bretagna

Tables Requisite to be Used with the Astronomical and Nautical Ephemeris

ISBN/EAN: 9783741140020

Manufactured in Europe, USA, Canada, Australia, Japa

Cover: Foto ©Thomas Meinert / pixelio.de

Manufactured and distributed by brebook publishing software
(www.brebook.com)

Gran Bretagna

Tables Requisite to be Used with the Astronomical and Nautical

Ephemeris

T A B L E S

Requisite to be used with the

ASTRONOMICAL AND NAUTICAL

E P H E M E R I S.

Published by Order of the

COMMISSIONERS OF LONGITUDE.

L O N D O N:

Printed by W. RICHARDSON and S. CLARK;

AND SOLD BY

J. NOURSE, Bookseller to his Majesty, in the Strand;
and Meſſ. MOUNT and PAGE, on Towerhill.

M DCC LXVI.

[Price 1s. 6d.]

A TABLE of the Refraction of the Heavenly Bodies in Altitude.

App. Alt.	Refrac.	App. Alt.	Refrac.	App. Alt.	Refr.	App. Alt.	Refr.	App. Alt.	Refr.
° '	' "	° '	' "	° '	' "	° '	' "	° '	' "
0. 0	33. 0	4. 50	10. 11	10. 30	5. 0	26. 0	1. 56	59. 0	0. 34
5	32. 10	5. 0	9. 54	10. 45	4. 53	27.	1. 51	60.	33
10	31. 22	5. 10	9. 38	11. 0	4. 47	28.	1. 47	61.	32
15	30 35	5. 20	9. 23	11. 15	4. 40	29.	1. 42	62.	31
20	29. 50	5. 30	9. 6	11. 30	4. 34	30.	1. 38	63.	29
30	28. 22	5. 40	8. 54	11. 45	4. 29	31.	1. 35	64.	28
35	28. 5	5. 50	8. 41	12. 0	4. 23	32.	1. 31	65.	26
40	27. 30	6. 0	8. 26	12. 20	4. 16	33.	1. 28	66.	25
45	27. 0	6. 10	8. 15	12. 40	4. 9	34.	1. 24	67.	24
50	25. 42	6. 20	8. 3	13. 0	4. 3	35.	1. 21	68.	23
1. 0	24. 29	6. 30	7. 51	13. 20	3. 57	36.	1. 18	69.	22
1. 10	23. 20	6. 40	7. 40	13. 40	3. 51	37.	1. 16	70.	21
1. 20	22. 15	6. 50	7. 30	14. 0	3. 45	38.	1. 13	71.	19
1. 30	21. 15	7. 0	7. 20	14. 20	3. 40	39.	1. 10	72.	18
1. 40	20. 18	7. 10	7. 11	14. 40	3. 35	40.	1. 8	73.	17
1. 50	19. 25	7. 20	7. 2	15. 0	3. 30	41.	1. 5	74.	16
2. 0	18. 35	7. 30	6. 53	15. 30	3. 24	42.	1. 3	75.	15
2. 10	17. 48	7. 40	6. 45	16. 0	3. 17	43.	1. 1	76.	14
2. 20	17. 4	7. 50	6. 37	16. 30	3. 10	44.	59	77.	13
2. 30	16. 24	8. 0	6. 29	17. 0	3. 4	45.	57	78.	12
2. 40	15. 45	8. 10	6. 22	17. 30	2. 59	46.	55	79.	11
2. 50	15. 0	8. 20	6. 15	18. 0	2. 54	47.	53	80.	10
3. 0	14. 36	8. 30	6. 8	18. 30	2. 49	48.	51	81.	9
3. 10	14. 4	8. 40	6. 1	19. 0	2. 44	49.	49	82.	8
3. 20	13. 34	8. 50	5. 55	19. 30	2. 39	50.	48	83.	7
3. 30	13. 0	9. 0	5. 48	20. 0	2. 35	51.	46	84.	6
3. 40	12. 45	9. 10	5. 42	20. 30	2. 31	52.	44	85.	5
3. 50	12. 15	9. 20	5. 36	21. 0	2. 27	53.	43	86.	4
4. 0	11. 51	9. 30	5. 31	21. 30	2. 24	54.	41	87.	3
4. 10	11. 20	9. 40	5. 25	22. 0	2. 20	55.	40	88.	2
4. 20	11. 8	9. 50	5. 20	23. 0	2. 14	56.	38	89.	1
4. 30	10. 45	10. 0	5. 15	24. 0	2. 7	57.	37	90.	0
4. 40	10. 29	10. 15	5. 7	25. 0	2. 2	58.	35		

A TABLE of the Moon's Parallax in Altitude.

App. Alt. of ☽	Horizontal Parallax of the Moon.									
°	53′	54′	55′	56′	57′	58′	59′	60′	6	
1	53′	54′	55′	56′	57′	58′	59′	60′		62
2	53	54	55	56	57	58	59	60		62
3	53	54	55	56	57	58	59	60	61	
4	53	54	55	56	57	58	59	60	61	
5	53	54	55	56	57	59	59	60	61	62
6	53	54	55	56	57	58	59	60	61	62
7	53	54	55	56	57	58	59	60	61	62
8	52	53	54	55	56	57	58	59	60	61
9	52	53	54	55	56	57	58	59	60	61
10	52	53	54	55	56	57	58	59	60	61
11	52	53	54	55	56	57	58	59	60	61
12	52	53	54	55	56	57	58	59	60	61
13	52	53	54	55	55	56	57	58	59	60
14	51	52	53	54	55	56	57	58	59	60
15	51	52	53	54	55	56	57	58	59	60
16	51	52	53	54	55	56	57	58	58	59
17	51	52	53	54	54	55	56	57	58	59
18	50	51	52	53	54	55	56	57	58	59
19	50	51	52	53	54	55	56	57	58	59
20	50	51	52	53	54	54	55	56	57	58
21	49	50	51	52	53	54	55	56	57	58
22	49	50	51	52	53	54	55	56	56	57
23	49	50	51	51	52	53	54	55	56	57
24	48	49	50	51	52	53	54	55	56	57
25	48	49	50	51	52	53	53	54	55	56
26	47	48	49	50	51	52	53	54	55	56
27	47	48	49	50	51	52	53	53	54	55
28	47	48	49	49	50	51	52	53	54	55
29	46	47	48	49	50	51	52	52	53	54
30	46	47	48	48	49	50	51	52	53	54

Continuation of the TABLE of the Moon's Parallax in Altitude.

App. Alt. of ☽	Horizontal Parallax of the Moon.									
°	53'	54'	55'	56'	57'	58'	59'	60'	61'	62'
31	45	45	47	48	49	50	51	51	52	53
32	45	46	47	47	48	49	50	51	52	53
33	44	45	46	47	48	49	49	50	51	52
34	44	45	46	46	47	48	49	50	51	52
35	43	44	45	46	47	47	48	49	50	51
36	43	44	44	45	45	47	48	48	49	50
37	42	43	44	45	45	46	47	48	49	50
38	42	43	43	44	45	46	46	47	48	49
39	41	42	43	43	44	45	46	47	47	48
40	40	41	42	43	44	44	45	46	47	48
41	40	41	41	42	43	44	44	45	46	47
42	39	40	41	42	42	43	44	45	45	46
43	38	39	40	41	42	42	43	44	45	46
44	38	39	40	40	41	42	42	43	44	45
45	37	38	39	40	40	41	42	43	43	44
46	36	37	38	39	40	40	41	42	42	43
47	36	37	38	38	39	40	40	41	42	43
48	35	36	37	37	38	39	39	40	41	42
49	34	35	36	37	37	38	39	39	40	41
50	34	35	35	36	37	37	38	39	39	40
51	33	34	35	35	36	36	37	38	38	39
52	32	33	34	34	35	36	36	37	38	39
53	31	32	33	34	34	35	35	36	37	38
54	31	32	32	33	33	34	35	35	36	37
55	30	31	31	32	33	33	34	34	35	36
56	29	30	31	31	32	32	33	34	34	35
57	28	29	30	30	31	32	32	33	33	34
58	28	29	29	30	30	31	31	32	32	33
59	27	28	28	29	29	30	30	31	31	32
60	26	27	27	28	28	29	29	30	30	30

Continuation of the T A B L E of the Moon's Parallax in Altitude.

App. Alt. of ☽	Horizontal Parallax of the Moon.									
P	53′	54′	55′	56′	57′	58′	59′	60′	61′	62′
61	26	26	27	27	28	28	29	29	30	30
62	25	25	26	26	27	27	28	28	29	29
63	24	24	25	25	26	26	27	27	28	28
64	24	24	24	24	25	25	26	26	27	27
65	23	23	23	24	24	24	25	25	26	26
66	22	22	22	23	23	24	24	24	25	25
67	21	21	21	22	22	23	23	23	24	24
68	20	20	21	21	21	22	22	22	23	23
69	19	19	20	20	20	21	21	21	22	22
70	18	18	19	19	19	20	20	20	21	21
71	18	18	18	18	19	19	19	19	20	20
72	17	17	17	17	18	18	18	18	19	19
73	16	16	16	16	17	17	17	17	18	18
74	15	15	15	15	16	16	16	16	17	17
75	14	14	14	14	15	15	15	15	16	16
76	13	13	13	14	14	14	14	14	15	15
77	12	12	12	13	13	13	13	13	14	14
78	11	11	11	12	12	12	12	12	13	13
79	10	10	10	11	11	11	11	11	12	12
80	9	9	10	10	10	10	10	10	11	11
81	8	8	9	9	9	9	9	9	10	10
82	7	7	8	8	8	8	8	8	9	9
83	7	7	7	7	7	7	7	7	8	8
84	6	6	6	6	6	6	6	6	7	7
85	5	5	5	5	5	5	5	5	5	5
86	4	4	4	4	4	4	4	4	4	4
87	3	3	3	3	3	3	3	3	3	3
88	2	2	2	2	2	2	2	2	2	2
89	1	1	1	1	1	1	1	1	1	1
90	0	0	0	0	0	0	0	0	0	0

A TABLE to turn Degrees and Minutes into Time, and the contrary.

D.	H. M.	D.	H. M.	D.	H. M.	D.	H. M.
M.	M. S.	M.	M. S.				
1	0. 4	31	2. 4	61	4. 4	91	6. 4
2	0. 8	32	2. 8	62	4. 6	92	6. 8
3	0. 12	33	2. 12	63	4. 12	93	6. 12
4	0. 16	34	2. 16	64	4. 16	94	6. 16
5	0. 20	35	2. 20	65	4. 20	95	6. 20
6	0. 24	36	2. 24	66	4. 24	96	6. 24
7	0. 28	37	2. 28	67	4. 28	97	6. 28
8	0. 32	38	2. 32	68	4. 32	98	6. 32
9	0. 36	39	2. 36	69	4. 36	99	6. 36
10	0. 40	40	2. 40	70	4. 40	100	6. 40
11	0. 44	41	2. 44	71	4. 44	101	6. 44
12	0. 48	42	2. 49	72	4. 48	102	6. 48
13	0. 52	43	2. 52	73	4. 52	103	6. 52
14	0. 56	44	2. 56	74	4. 56	104	6. 56
15	1. 0	45	3. 0	75	5. 0	105	7. 0
16	1. 4	46	3. 4	76	5. 4	106	7. 4
17	1. 8	47	3. 8	77	5. 8	107	7. 8
18	1. 12	48	3. 12	78	5. 12	108	7. 12
19	1. 16	49	3. 16	79	5. 16	109	7. 16
20	1. 20	50	3. 20	80	5. 20	110	7. 20
21	1. 24	51	3. 24	81	5. 24	111	7. 24
22	1. 28	52	3. 28	82	5. 28	112	7. 28
23	1. 32	53	3. 32	83	5. 32	113	7. 32
24	1. 36	54	3. 36	84	5. 36	114	7. 36
25	1. 40	55	3. 40	85	5. 40	115	7. 40
26	1. 44	56	3. 44	86	5. 44	116	7. 44
27	1. 48	57	3. 48	87	5. 48	117	7. 48
28	1. 52	58	3. 52	88	5. 52	118	7. 52
29	1. 56	59	3. 56	89	5. 56	119	7. 56
30	2. 0	60	4. 0	90	6. 0	120	8. 0

Continuation of the TABLE for turning Degrees and Minutes into Time, and the contrary.

D.	H. M.	D.	H. M.	D.	H. M.	D.	H. M.
121	8. 4	151	10. 4	181	12. 4	211	14. 4
122	8. 8	152	10. 8	182	12. 8	212	14. 8
123	8.12	153	10.12	183	12.12	213	14.12
124	8.16	154	10.16	184	12.16	214	14.16
125	8.20	155	10.20	185	12.20	215	14.20
126	8.24	156	10.24	186	12.24	216	14.24
127	8.28	157	10.28	187	12.28	217	14.28
128	8.32	158	10.32	188	12.32	218	14.32
129	8.36	159	10.36	189	12.36	219	14.36
130	8.40	160	10.40	190	12.40	220	14.40
131	8.44	161	10.44	191	12.44	221	14.44
132	8.48	162	10.48	192	12.48	222	14.48
133	8.52	163	10.52	193	12.52	223	14.52
134	8.56	164	10.56	194	12.56	224	14.56
135	9. 0	165	11. 0	195	13. 0	225	15. 0
136	9. 4	166	11. 4	196	13. 4	226	15. 4
137	9. 8	167	11. 8	197	13. 8	227	15. 8
138	9.12	168	11.12	198	13.12	228	15.12
139	9.16	169	11.16	199	13.16	229	15.16
140	9.20	170	11.20	200	13.20	230	15.20
141	9.24	171	11.24	201	13.24	231	15.24
142	9.28	172	11.28	202	13.28	232	15.28
143	9.32	173	11.32	203	13.32	233	15.32
144	9.36	174	11.36	204	13.36	234	15.36
145	9.40	175	11.40	205	13.40	235	15.40
146	9.44	176	11.44	206	13.44	236	15.44
147	9.48	177	11.48	207	13.48	237	15.48
148	9.52	178	11.52	208	13.52	238	15.52
149	9.56	179	11.56	209	13.56	239	15.56
150	10. 0	180	12. 0	210	14. 0	240	16. 0

Continuation of the TABLE for turning Degrees and Minutes into Time; and the contrary.

D.	H. M.	D.	H. M.	D.	H. M.	D.	H. M.
241	16. 4	271	18. 4	301	20. 4	331	22. 4
242	16. 8	272	18. 8	302	20. 8	332	22. 8
243	16. 12	273	18. 12	303	20. 12	333	22. 12
244	16. 16	274	18. 16	304	20. 16	334	22. 16
245	16. 20	275	18. 20	305	20. 20	335	22. 20
246	16. 24	276	18. 24	306	20. 24	336	22. 24
247	16. 28	277	18. 28	307	20. 28	337	22. 28
248	16. 32	278	18. 32	308	20. 32	338	22. 32
249	16. 36	279	18. 36	309	20. 36	339	22. 36
250	16. 40	280	18. 40	310	20. 40	340	22. 40
251	16. 44	281	18. 44	311	20. 44	341	22. 44
252	16. 48	282	18. 48	312	20. 48	342	22. 48
253	16. 52	283	18. 52	313	20. 52	343	22. 52
254	16. 56	284	18. 56	314	20. 56	344	22. 56
255	17. 0	285	19. 0	315	21. 0	345	23. 0
256	17. 4	286	19. 4	316	21. 4	346	23. 4
257	17. 8	287	19. 8	317	21. 8	347	23. 8
258	17. 12	288	19. 12	318	21. 12	348	23. 12
259	17. 16	289	19. 16	319	21. 16	349	23. 16
260	17. 20	290	19. 20	320	21. 20	350	23. 20
261	17. 24	291	19. 24	321	21. 24	351	23. 24
262	17. 28	292	19. 28	322	21. 28	352	23. 28
263	17. 32	293	19. 32	323	21. 32	353	23. 32
264	17. 36	294	19. 36	324	21. 36	354	23. 36
265	17. 40	295	19. 40	325	21. 40	355	23. 40
266	17. 44	296	19. 44	326	21. 44	356	23. 44
267	17. 48	297	19. 48	327	21. 48	357	23. 48
268	17. 52	298	19. 52	328	21. 52	358	23. 52
269	17. 56	299	19. 56	329	21. 56	359	23. 56
270	18. 0	300	20. 0	330	22. 0	360	24. 0

A CORRECT TABLE.

OF THE

Longitude and Latitude of the principal Zodiacal Stars proper to take the Moon's Distance from, for finding the Longitude at Sea.
Deduced from Dr. Bradley's Observations.

Beginning of 1767.	Mag-nitud.	Longitude. S. ° ′ ″	Latitude. ° ′ ″
γ Pegasi ———	2	♈ 5. 54. 38	12. 35. 35 N
* α Arietis ———	2	1. 4. 24. 20	9. 57. 30 N
α Ceti — —	2	1. 11. 3. 56	12. 36. 16 S
* .Aldebaran ———	1	2. 6. 32. 3	5. 29. 2 S
β Tauri ———	2	2. 19. 19. 19	5. 21. 59 N
α Orionis ———	1	2. 25. 30. 5	16. 3. 31 S
* Pollux — —	1. 2	3. 20. 0. 16	6. 40. 5 N
Procyon ———	1	3. 22. 34. 29	15. 58. 8 S
* Regulus ———	1	4. 26. 35. 31	0. 27. 27 N
β Leonis ———	2	5. 18. 23. 9	12. 17. 8 N
* Spica Virginis—	1	6. 20. 35. 31	2. 2. 11 S
α Libræ ———	2	7. 11. 50. 11	0. 21. 48 N
β Libræ ———	2	7. 16. 7. 23	8. 31. 32 N
* Antares ———	1	8. 6. 30. 40	4. 32. 17 S
γ Sagittarii ———	2. 3	9. 9. 7. 59	3. 24. 55 S
* α Aquilæ ———	1	9. 28. 29. 13	29. 18. 36 N
* β Capricorni —	3	10. 0. 47. 37	4. 36. 46 N
* Fomalhaut ———	1	11. 0. 34. 47	21. 6. 28 S
* α Pegasi ———	2	11. 20. 14. 30	19. 24. 38 N

N. B. Those Stars only marked with Asterisks are made use of in the Distances of the Astronomical and Nautical Ephemeris.

TABLE to find the Aberration of a Zodiacal Star in Longitude.

Aberration ✳ in Longitude.			
Arg. Long. ☉ —— Long. ✳			
Sign.	0	1	2
Sig.	6 +	7 +	8 +
0	"	"	"	o
0	20	17	10	30
3	20	17	9	27
6	20	16	8	24
9	20	16	7	21
12	20	15	6	18
15	19	14	5	15
18	19	13	4	12
21	19	13	3	9
24	18	12	2	6
27	19	11	1	3
30	17	10	0	0
Sig.	11	10	9
Sig.	5 +	4 +	3 +

A particular Table of Limits for α Aquilæ.

☽ Lat. N.	Dif. of Lon. ☽ & α Aqui.	☽ Lat. S.	Dif. of Lon. ☽ & α Aqui.
o	o '	o	o '
0	48. 26	0	48. 26
1	47. 15	1	49. 45
2	45. 43	2	51. 3
3	44. 11	3	52. 10
4	42. 43	4	53. 21
5	41. 10	5	54. 26
0. 20	20. 28	0. 0	54. 46

A TABLE for chusing proper Stars for observing the Moon's Dist. from.

Dif. or Sum of ☽ & ✳ Lats.	Dif. of Lon. of ☽ & ✳.
o	o '
1	10. 0
2	10.
3	10.
4	10.
5	10.
6	10. 57
7	12. 49
8	14. 42
9	16. 37
10	18. 34
11	20. 33
12	22. 35
13	24. 39
14	26. 46
15	28. 57
16	31. 12
17	33. 31
18	35. 56
19	38. 28
20	41. 6
21	43. 54
22	46. 52
23	50. 3
24	53. 32
25	57. 23
26	61. 49
27	65. 58
28	73. 48

A TABLE for finding the Correction of the Moon's Longitude or Latitude, obtained by Proportion from the Places calculated for Noon and Midnight.

App. Time after Noon or Midnight.	Second Difference of Moon's Place.										App. Time after Noon or Midnight.
	1'	2'	3'	4'	5'	6'	7'	8'	9'	10'	
H. M.	"	"	"	"	"	"	"	"	"	"	H. M.
0. 0	0	0	0	0	0	0	0	0	0	0	12. 0
0. 10	0	1	1	2	2	2	3	3	4	4	11. 50
0. 20	1	2	2	3	4	5	6	6	7	8	11. 40
0. 30	1	2	4	5	6	7	8	10	11	12	11. 30
0. 40	2	3	5	6	8	9	11	13	14	16	11. 20
0. 50	2	4	6	8	10	12	13	15	17	19	11. 10
1. 0	2	5	7	9	11	14	16	18	21	23	11. 0
1. 10	3	5	8	10	13	16	18	21	24	26	10. 50
1. 20	3	6	9	12	15	18	21	24	27	30	10. 40
1. 30	3	6	10	13	16	20	23	26	29	33	10. 30
1. 40	4	7	11	14	18	21	25	29	32	36	10. 20
1. 50	4	8	12	15	19	23	27	31	35	39	10. 10
2. 0	4	8	12	17	21	25	29	33	37	42	10. 0
2. 10	4	9	13	18	22	27	31	35	40	44	9. 50
2. 20	5	9	14	19	23	28	33	38	42	47	9. 40
2. 30	5	10	15	20	25	30	34	39	44	49	9. 30
2. 40	5	10	15	21	26	31	36	41	47	52	9. 20
2. 50	5	11	16	22	27	32	38	43	49	54	9. 10
3. 0	6	11	17	23	28	34	39	45	51	56	9. 0
3. 10	6	12	17	23	29	35	41	46	52	58	8. 50
3. 20	6	12	18	24	30	36	42	48	54	60	8. 40
3. 30	6	12	18	25	31	37	43	49	56	62	8. 30
3. 40	6	13	19	25	32	38	45	51	57	64	8. 20
3. 50	6	13	19	26	33	39	46	52	59	65	8. 10
4. 0	7	13	20	27	33	40	47	53	60	67	8. 0
4. 10	7	14	20	27	34	41	47	54	61	68	7. 50
4. 20	7	14	21	28	35	41	48	55	62	69	7. 40
4. 30	7	14	21	28	35	42	49	56	63	70	7. 30
4. 40	7	14	21	28	36	43	50	57	64	71	7. 20
4. 50	7	14	22	29	36	43	50	58	65	72	7. 10
5. 0	7	15	22	29	36	44	51	58	66	73	7. 0
5. 30	7	15	22	30	37	45	52	60	67	74	6. 30
6. 0	7	15	22	30	37	45	52	60	67	75	6. 0

Add the Correction to the Moon's Longitude or Latitude, when the Motion in 12 Hours is decreasing; and subtract it from the same, when the Motion in 12 Hours is increasing.

A Catalogue of the Right Ascensions and Declinations of the principal fixed Stars of the first and second Magnitude, adapted to the Year 1760, with their Variations in Ten Years.

Names of the Stars	Character	Magnitude	Rt. Ascension ° '	Rt. Ascen. Increase in 10 Years ' ''	Declination	Decl. incre. or diminish in 10 Years
Extremity of the Wing of Pegasus, Algenib,	γ	2	0.19	7.42	13.54 N	+3.20
In the Head of the Phœnix,	α	2	3.41	7.30	43.34 S	—3.20
The bright Star in the Tail of the Whale,	β	2	7.59	7.33	19.15 S	—3.18
In the Girdle of Andromeda,	β	2	14.11	8.14	34.23 N	+3.14
The Spring of the River Eridanus, Achernar,	α	1	22.15	5.37	58.25 S	—3.5
In the Jaw of the Whale,	α	2	42.32	7.49	3.10 N	+2.28
In the Head of Medusa, Algol,	β	2	43.7	9.36	40.3 N	+2.26
The bright Star of Perseus,	α	2	46.58	10.29	47.1 N	+2.17
The South Eye of the Bull, Aldebaran,	α	1	65.39	8.34	16.1 N	+1.23
The bright Star in the Left Shoulder of Auriga, Capella,	α	1	74.52	11.0	45.44 N	+0.53
The bright Foot of Orion, Rigel,	β	1	75.44	7.12	8.29 S	—0.50
The North Horn of the Bull,	β	2	77.44	9.27	28.23 N	+0.43
The Western Shoulder of Orion,	γ	2	78.10	8.3	6.7 N	+0.42
Bright Star in the Dove,	α	2	82.48	5.30	34.13 S	—0.25
The Eastern Shoulder of Orion,	α	1	85.39	8.7	7.21 N	+0.16
The bright Star in the Poop of the Ship Argo, Canobus,	α	1	94.42	3.21	52.34 S	+0.16
The bright Star in the Dog's Mouth, Sirius,	α	1	98.44	6.43	16.24 S	+0.30
In the Head of the Northern Twin, Castor,	α	1	102.55	9.41	32.23 N	—1.7
The little Dog, Procyon,	α	1	111.47	9.0	5.49 N	—1.13
In the Head of the Southern Twin, Pollux,	β	1	112.46	9.23	28.35 N	—1.17

Name						
The bright Star in the Oars of the Ship Argo,	β	1	137. 0	1.52	68.45 S	+2.28
The Heart of the Female Hydra,	α	2	130. 3	7.24	7.40 S	+2.31
The Lion's Heart, *Regulus*,	α	1	148.59	8. 6	13. 5 N	−2.51
Northermost Star in the Square of the great Bear,	α	2	162.17	9.44	63. 0 N	−3.10
The Lion's Tail,	β	2	174.18	7.43	15.52 N	−3.19
Southermost Star of the Crofiers, or the Foot of the Crofs,	α	1	183.28	8. 3	61.49 S	+3.20
The Virgin's Spike,	α	1	198.15	7.54	9.56 S	+3.10
The laft Star in the Tail of the great Bear,	β	2	204.35	6. 1	50.29 N	−3. 2
The Weftermoft Foot of the Centaur,	β	2	206.54	10.13	59.14 S	+2.59
The bright Star in Bootes, *Arcturus*,	α	1	211.15	7. 3	20.24 N	−2.52
The bright Star in the Eaftern Foot of the Centaur,	β	1	216. 1	11. 1	59.52 S	+2.42
The Southern Scale of Libra,	α	2	219.31	8.16	16. 4 S	+2.35
The Northern Star of Libra,	β	2	226. 8	8. 3	8.31 S	+2.20
The bright Star of the Crown,	β	3	231.14	6.20	27.30 N	−2. 6
The Northermoft Star of the Scorpion's Forehead,	α	2	237.59	8.40	19. 8 S	+1.47
The Scorpion's Heart, *Antares*,	α	1	243.47	0. 8	25.53 S	+1.29
In the Eaftern Knee of Ophiuchus,	α	2	254.16	8.36	15.25 S	+0.55
The Head of Ophiuchus,	α	2	261. 2	6.57	12.45 N	−0.32
The bright Star of the Harp, *Lyra*,	α	1	277.16	5. 3	38.35 N	+0.25
The bright Star of the Eagle, *Atair*,	α	3	294.52	7.15	8.16 N	+1.23
The Eye of the Peacock,	α	2	301.47	12.13	57.28 S	−1.44
The Tail of the Swan,	α	2	308.22	5. 7	44.27 N	+2. 4
The Weftermoft Wing of the Crane,	α	2	328.23	9.56	48. 4 S	−2.50
In the Mouth of the Southern Fifh, *Fomalhaut*,	β	1	341.11	8.21	30.51 S	−1. 9
In the Shoulder of Pegasus,	α	2	343. 8	7.12	26.50 N	+3.11
In the Wing of Pegasus, *Merkab*,	β	1	343.18	7.27	13.58 N	+3.13
The Head of Andromeda,	α	2	359. 6	7.43	27.48 N	+3.20

A TABLE of the Multipliers of the Difference between the Moon's Longitude computed, and that inferred from Observation, to find the Error of the Ship's Account in Longitude.

Enter with hourly Motion of ☽, or Difference of hourly Motions of ☉ and ☽, according as ☽'s Distance is taken from a Star or the Sun.

Ho. Mo. ☽ or diffe. Ho. Mo. ☉ & ☽	Multipliers.	Ho. Mo. ☽ or diffe. Ho. Mo. ☉ & ☽	Multipliers.
′ ″		′ ″	
25.45	35,0		
25. 0	34,6	32. 0	28,1
26.15	34,3	32.15	27,9
26.30	34,0	32.30	27,7
26.45	33,6	32.45	27,5
27. 0	33,3	33. 0	27,3
27.15	33,0	33.15	27,1
27.30	32,7	33.30	26,9
27.45	32,4	33.45	26,7
28. 0	32,1	34. 0	26,5
28.15	31,8	34.15	26,3
28.30	31,6	34.30	26,1
28.45	31,3	34.45	25,9
29. 0	31,0	35. 0	25,7
29.15	30,8	35.15	25,5
29.30	30,5	35.30	25,3
29.45	30,2	35.45	25,2
30. 0	30,0	36. 0	25,0
30.15	29,7	36.15	24,8
30.30	29,5	36.30	24,7
30.45	29,3	36.45	24,5
31. 0	29,0	37. 0	24,3
31.15	28,8	37.15	24,2
31.30	28,6	37.30	24,0
31.45	28,3	37.45	23,8
		38. 0	23,7

A TABLE of the Depression or Dip of the Horizon of the Sea.

Elevation of the Eye above the Sea in Feet.	Depression of the Horizon of the Sea. ′ ″
1	0.57
2	1.21
3	1.39
4	1.55
5	2. 8
6	2.20
7	2.31
8	2.42
9	2.52
10	3. 1
12	3.18
14	3.34
16	3.49
18	4. 3
20	4.16
22	4.28
24	4.40
26	4.52
28	5. 3
30	5.14
35	5.39
40	6. 2
45	6.24
50	6.44
60	7.23
70	7.59
80	8.32
90	9. 3
100	9.33

[15]

. Right Afcenfions and Declinations of fome of the
principal fixed Stars.

Deduced from Dr. Bradley's Obfervations.

Jan. 1, 1767. Stars Names.	Right Afcenfions.	Ann. Varia. in A.R.	Declination.	Ann. Variation in Declination.	Magnitudes.
	° ′ ″	″	° ′ ″	′	
γ Pegafi ———	0. 18. 58,4	46,20	13. 53. 15,3 N	+20,04	2
α Arietis ———	28. 31. 18,4	50,06	22. 21. 02,5 N	+17,64	2
α Ceti ———	42. 31. 53,1	46,93	3. 9. 44,1 N	+14,80	2
Aldebaran —	65. 38. 36,6	51,41	16. 1. 18,1 N	+ 8,32	1
Capella ———	74. 52. 41,7	66,03	45. 43. 39,0 N	+ 5,28	1
Rigel ———	75. 50. 13,8	43,30	8. 29. 15,4 S	— 4,94	1
β Tauri ———	77. 53. 44,6	56,80	28. 23. 17,7 N	+ 4,24	2
α Orionis ———	85. 38. 28,4	48,75	7. 20. 35,9 N	+ 1,56	1
Sirius ———	98. 43. 19,2	40,35	16. 24. 28,1 S	+ 3,10	1
Caftor ———	109. 55. 32,8	58,15	32. 22. 36,4 N	— 6,80	2
Procyon ———	111. 46. 33,3	48,08	5. 48. 32,1 N	— 7,42	1
Pollux———	112. 45. 37,6	56,27	28. 34. 9,1 N	— 7,72	2
Regulus — —	148. 59. 12,7	48,60	13. 5. 49,6 N	—17,17	1
Spica Virginis	198. 14. 15,0	47,27	9. 56. 17,0 S	+18,97	1
Arcturus ———	211. 15. 49,2	42,32	20. 24. 31,9 N	—17,16	1
Antares — —	243. 47. 25,3	54,92	25. 53. 36,3 S	+ 8,89	1
ι Sagittarii———	272. 10. 43,6	59,95	34. 28. 7,5 S	— 0,72	2
α Aquilæ———	294. 51. 5,6	43,54	8. 16. 3,8 N	+ 8,40	1
2 α Capricorni	301. 16. 42,4	50,20	13. 15. 0,2 S	—10,40	3
Fomalhaut.—	341. 10. 55,5	50,67	30. 51. 1,2 S	—18,97	1
α Pegafi ———	343. 17. 35,7	44,75	13. 57. 20,4 N	+19,20	2

Longitudes and Latitudes of some of the principal fixed Stars.

Deduced from Dr. Bradley's Observations.

Jan. 1, 1767. Stars Names.	Longitude. °　′　″	Latitude. °　′　″	Magnitudes
γ Pegasi ———	♈ 5. 54. 38,5	12. 35. 34,5 N	2
α Aurigæ ———	♉ 4. 24. 20,0	9. 57. 37,0 N	2
α Ceti ———	♉ 11. 3. 56,0	12. 36. 16,0 S	2
Aldebaran —	♊ 6. 32. 02,5	5. 29. 02,0 S	1
Rigel ———	13. 34. 26,0	31. 9. 10,0 S	1
Capella ———	18. 36. 11,0	22. 51. 46,0 N	1
β Tauri ———	19. 19. 19,0	5. 21. 59,0 N	2
α Orionis ———	25. 30. 05,0	16. 3. 31,0 S	1
Sirius ———	♋ 10. 52. 26,0	39. 32. 55,0 S	1
Castor — —	16. 39. 51,0	10. 4. 35,0 N	2
Pollux — —	20. 0. 16,0	6. 40. 04,5 N	2
Procyon —	22. 34. 29,5	15. 58. 08,0 S	1
Regulus ———	♌ 26. 35. 31,0	0. 27. 27,0 N	1
Spica Virginis	♎ 20. 35. 32,0	2. 2. 11,0 S	1
Arcturus ———	20. 59. 04,0	30. 54. 10,5 N	1
Antares ———	♐ 6. 30. 40,0	4. 32. 17,0 S	1
α Sagittarii —	♑ 1. 49. 47,0	11. 0. 45,0 S	2
α Aquilæ —	28. 29. 13,0	29. 18. 36,0 N	1
2 α Capricorni	♒ 0. 36. 19,0	6. 57. 16,0 N	3
Fomalhaut —	♓ 0. 34. 47,0	21. 6. 28,0 S	1
α Pegasi ———	20. 14. 30,0	19. 24. 37,5 N	2

NEW

TABLES

AND

RULES

FOR CORRECTING THE

APPARENT DISTANCE

OF THE

MOON FROM THE SUN

OR A

FIXED STAR,

ON ACCOUNT OF

REFRACTION AND PARALLAX.

BY MR. LYONS.

C

A TABLE into Seconds, and the contrary.

′	″	′	″	′	″	′	″
,01	1	,61	37	,76	46	,91	55
,02	1	,62	37	,77	46	,92	55
,03	2	,63	38	,78	47	,93	56
,04	2	,64	38	,79	47	,94	56
,05	3	,65	39	,80	48	,95	57
,06	4	,66	40	,81	49	,96	58
,07	4	,67	40	,82	49	,97	58
,08	5	,68	41	,83	50	,98	59
,09	5	,69	41	,84	50	,99	59

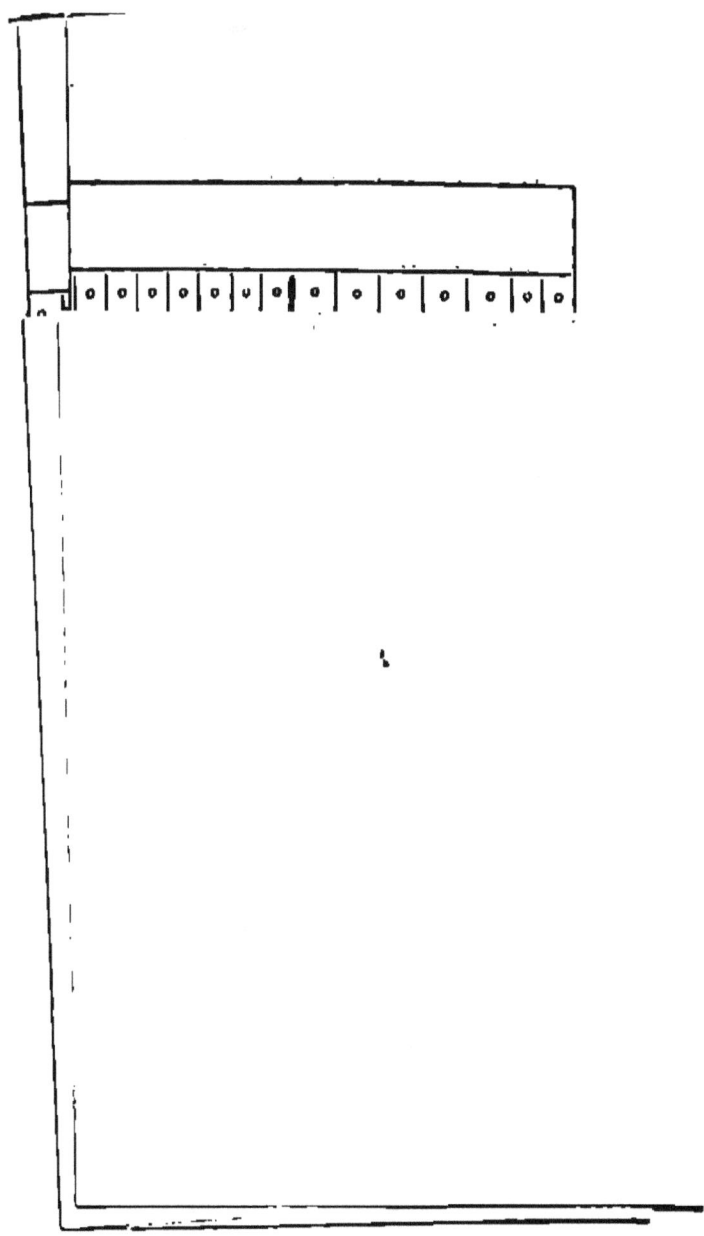

U S E

OF THE PRECEDING

T A B L E S,

WITH

R U L E S

TO CLEAR THE

APPARENT DISTANCE

OF THE

MOON FROM A STAR,

OF THE EFFECTS OF

REFRACTION AND PARALLAX.

To find the Effect of Refraction.

IN Table I. find what Number anfwers to the two Altitudes of the Moon and Star, the leffer of the two Altitudes
being found at the Top of the Table, the other in the firft
Column on the left Hand.

Prefix the Index 2 to this Number (confidered as the decimal Part of a Logarithm) and add it to the logarithmic Cofecant of the apparent Diftance of the Moon and Star; and,
abating 10 from the Index of the Sum, find what natural
Number anfwers to it in the Table of Logarithms.

From this Number fubftract that correfponding to the given
Diftance, and to the leffer of the two Altitudes in Table II.
if the Diftance is lefs than 90°; or add them together, if the
Diftance exceeds 90°; the Remainder or Sum is the Effect

C 2   of

of Refraction in Seconds; which added to the obferved Diftance, gives the Diftance cleared of Refraction.

In any of the Cafes falling on the right Hand of the black waving Line, or if both Altitudes exceed 50°, the Effect of Refraction may be had at once by Table III.

To find the Effect of Parallax.

Add together the proportional Logarithm of the Moon's horizontal Parallax, the logarithmic Cofecant of the Star's Altitude corrected for Refraction, and the logarithmic Sine of the Diftance cleared from Refraction; the Sum, abating 20 from the Index, will be the proportional Logarithm of a firft Arc.

Add together the proportional Logarithm of the Moon's horizontal Parallax, the logarithmic Cofecant of the Moon's Altitude corrected for Refraction, and the Tangent of the Diftance cleared from Refraction; the Sum, abating 20 from the Index, will be the proportional Logarithm of a fecond Arc.

Then, if the Diftance is lefs than 90°, the Difference of thefe two Arcs is the principal Effect of Parallax (or Parallax in Diftance); which added to or fubftracted from the Diftance corrected for Refraction, according as the firft Arc is lefs or greater than the fecond, will give the Diftance corrected for the principal Effect of Parallax.

But if the Diftance exceeds 90°, the Sum of the two Arcs is to be taken inftead of their Difference, and is to be fubftracted from the Diftance corrected for Refraction.

In Table IV. in the Column marked above with the Diftance, find the two Numbers anfwering to the Parallax in Diftance and in Altitude; their Difference is the fecond Correction of Parallax in Seconds; which, added to or fubftracted from the Diftance corrected for Refraction and principal Effect of Parallax, according as the Diftance is lefs or greater than 90°, will give the correct or reduced Diftance.

EXAMPLE

Example I.

Let the apparent Altitude of the Star be . .	° ´ ´´	The Moon's horizontal Parallax . . .	´ ´´
Of the Moon's Centre	24. 48.	And consequently Parallax in Altitude, by p. 3d of Tables, is	56. 15
Observed Distance of the Moon's Centre from the Star . . .	12. 30. 51. 28. 35		55.

In Table I. the Number answering to 24°, and 12° of Altitude is 1411, and to 25 and 12 of Altitude is 1511; therefore 1° Increase of the greater Altitude produces an Increase of 100 in the tabular Number. Say then, by the Rule of Three, If 1° or 60´ give 100, what will 48´ (the Excess of the greater Altitude above 24°) give? the Answer is, 80; which, added to 1411, gives 1491, the Number corrected for exceeding Minutes of greater Altitude. Moreover, 24° and 12° of Altitude giving 1411, as above, and 24 and 13 giving 1232; therefore, 1° Increase of the lesser Altitude gives 179 Decrease of the tabular Number. Say therefore, by the Rule of Three, If 1° or 60´ give 179, what will 30´ (the Excess of the lesser Altitude above 12°) give? the Answer is, 89; which, subtracted from 1491 (the tabular Number corrected for exceeding Minutes of greater Altitude) leaves 1402 for the tabular Number corrected also for the exceeding Minutes of the lesser Altitude;

To which prefixing the Index 2, it will be . 2.1402
Log. Cosec. observed Distance 51°. 28´ . . 10.1066

12.2468

Rejecting 10 from the Index, we have 2.2468, which is the Logarithm of 176´´.

In Table II. under the Column intituled 10° and above, answering to the Distance 51° is 90´´, and answering to 52° is 86´´; therefore to 51°. 28´ there answers 88´´; which subtracted from 176´´, leaves the Effect of Refraction 88´´.

	° ´ ´´
Observed Distance	51. 28. 35
Effect of Refraction	+ 1. 28
Distance cleared of Refraction . . .	51. 30. 3

For

For Parallax.

App. Alt. of the Star	° ′ 24. 48	App. Alt. of the Moon	° ′ 12. 30
Refraction in Alt. fubftr.	2	Refraction in Alt. fubftr.	4
Alt. corr. for Refraction	24. 46	Alt. corr. for Refraction	12. 26
Cofecant 24. 46	. 10.3778	Cofecant . 12. 26 .	10.6669
Sine dift. 51. 30	9.8935	Tang. dift. 51. 30 .	10.0994
Proportional Log. of horizontal Paral- lax 56′. 15″ .	0.5051	Proportional Log. of horizontal Paral- lax 56′. 15″ .	0.5051
	20.9214		21.2714

Rejecting 20 from thefe Sums,

The Arc anfwering to the propor. Log. 9214 is 30. ′7 ″
2.2714 is 9. 38

Their Difference 20. 29 is
the principal Effect of Parallax, or Parallax in Diftance, to
be fubftracted; becaufe the firft Arc is greater than the fecond.

Diftance correfted for Refraction 51. 30. 3
Parallax in Diftance . . . . — 20. 29

Diftance correfted for Refrafit. and Par. in Dift. 51. 9. 34

In Table IV. under 51°, and againft 55′ the Parallax in
Altitude is 20″; in the fame Column againft 20′ the Parallax in Diftance is 3″; which fubftrafted from 20″, leaves
17″, for the fecond Correfition of Parallax, to be added:

° ′ ″
51. 9. 34
+ . 17

Reduced Dift. cleared both of Refr. and Par. . 51. 9. 51

N. B. The proportional Parts for the Minutes of the two
Altitudes in Table I. may be found alfo by the Rule of
Practice, or by Decimal Multiplication, as well as by the
Rule of Three. Thus, to find the proportional Part anfwer-
ing

ing to 48', the Excefs of the greater Altitude above 48°, I find, by the Rule of Practice, if 1°, or 60', give the Difference 100, 30' will give 50, 15' will give 25, and 3' will give 5; therefore 48' will give 30 + 15 + 5 = 80, as before. Or, by Decimal Multiplication, confidering that 48' is $\frac{8}{10}$ of 60', I multiply the Difference 100 by $\frac{8}{10}$, which gives the Product 80, as before. The decimal Part any Number of Minutes is of 60', may be feen at one Corner of Table I. againft the given Number of Minutes found in the Column there marked for Seconds.

EXAMPLE II.

Let apparent Alt. of the Star be $\left.\begin{array}{c}\\ \\ \end{array}\right\}$ 15: 25. — The Moon's horizontal Parallax . . $\left.\begin{array}{c}\\ \\ \end{array}\right\}$ 57. 3

Of the Moon's Centre 27. 30. — Whence the Parallax in Altitude, by p. 3d $\left.\begin{array}{c}\\ \\ \end{array}\right\}$ 51.

Ap. Dift. of the Star from the Moon's Centre . . $\left.\begin{array}{c}\\ \\ \end{array}\right\}$ 102. 30. 0

The Number in Table I. for the Altitudes 27° and 15° is 1176, the Difference for 1° Increase of the greater Altitude being + 75, and of the leffer Altitude — 123; whence the Correction for the Excefs 30' of the greater Altitude is + 37, and the Correction for the Excefs 25' of the leffer Altitude is — 51.

Whence the Number from Table I. corrected, is 1176 + 37 — 51 = 1162, or prefixing the Index 2, is . . . . $\left.\begin{array}{c}\\ \\ \end{array}\right\}$ 2.1162

Cofecant of Dift. 102°. 30' = Cofecant 77°. 30', the Supplement to 180° . . . . $\left.\begin{array}{c}\\ \\ \end{array}\right\}$ 10.0104

————

12.1266

Rejecting 10 from the Index, is Log. of . 134
Number in Table II. to be added, becaufe Diftance is above 99° . . $\left.\begin{array}{c}\\ \\ \end{array}\right\}$ + 25

————

Effect of Refraction . . . . 159 = 2'. 39"

Observed Diftance 102. 30. 0
Effect of Refraction . . . . + 2. 39

————

Diftance cleared of Refraction 102. 32. 39

For

For Parallax.

Prop. Log. of horiz. Parallax 57'. 3"	0.4990	Propor. Log. of the Moon's hor. Par. 57'. 3"	0.4990
Cofec. of the Star's app. Alt. 15°. 25' — Refract. 3' = 15°. 22'	10.5768	Cofec. of the Moon's app. Alt. 27°. 30' — Refract. 2' = 27°. 28'	10.3356
Sine Dift. cleared of Refrac. 102°. 33' or 77°. 27', its Supplem. to 180°	9.9895	Tang. Dift. clear of Refrac. 102°. 33' or 77°. 27', its Supplem. to 180°.	10.6524
Prop. Log. of 15'. 32" or Arc 1ft	20.0653	Prop. Log. of 5'. 52" or Arc 2d	21.4870
Arc 2d to be added, because Dift. is above 90°	+5.52		
Principal Effect of Par. or Par. in Dift.	21.24		

In Table IV. Parallax in Altitude 51' gives 5"
Parallax in Diflance 21 . . 1

Difference 4

Diflance cleared of Refraction . . . . . 102°. 52'. 39"
Parallax in Diflance to be fubftracted, becaufe
Diflance is above 90° . . . . — 21.24

102. 11. 15

Second Correction of Parallax to be fubftracted,
becaufe Diflance is above 90° . . . . . — 4

Diflance reduced, or cleared both of Refraction
and Parallax 102. 11. 11

EXAMPLE

Example III.

Let app. Alt. of the Star be . } 48. 20.		The horizontal Parallax . . . } 0, 55. 29		
Of the Moon . . 64. 30.		Whence the Par. in Altitude . } 0. 23.		
The obſerved Diſt. 33. 15.		The Star's Alt. corrected by Refr. } 48. 19.		
Effect of Refract. by Table III. } + 0. 34		The Moon's Alt. corr. by Refr. } 64. 30.		
Diſtance cleared of Refraction . } 33. 15. 34				

Prop. Log. hor. Par. 0.5111		Prop. Log. hor. Par. 0.5111		
Cofecant of the Star's Alt. corrected by Refract. 48°. 19′ } 10.1268		Cofec. of the Moon's Alt. corrected by Refract. 64°. 30′ } 10.0449		
Sine Diſt. 33°. 16′ . 9.7392		Tang. Diſt. 33°. 16′ 9.8169		
Prop. Log. Arc firſt 75′. 32″ . . } 20.3771		20.3715		
		Prop. Log. Arc 2d } 76. 20		
		Arc firſt . . 75. 32		
		Par. in Diſt. 0. 48		

Table IV. Parallax in Altitude 23′ gives 7″
Parallax in Diſtance 1 . . 0

Second Correction of Parallax. 7

Diſtance cleared of Refraction . . : 33. 15. 34
Parallax in Diſtance . . . . + 0. 48

33. 16. 22
Second Correction of Parallax . . . . + 7

Diſtance reduced 33. 16. 29

EXAMPLE IV.

Let the app. Alt. of the Star be	53. 13	The Moon's horizontal Parallax . .	61. 9	
Of the Moon .	64. 38	Whence the Moon's Parallax in Altitude	26. 0	

The app. Diſtance 56. 17. 44
Table LIL . . . + 1. 1

Diſtance cleared of Refraction } 56. 18. 45

Propor. Log. of the Moon's horizontal Parallax 61′. 9″	0.4689	Propor. Log. of the Moon's horizontal Parallax 61′. 9″	0.4689
Cofecant of the Star's Alt. corrected by Refract. 53°. 12′	10.0965	Cofec. of the Moon's Altitude corrected 64°. 38′ .	10.0449
Sine Diſt. cleared of Refract. 56°. 19′	9.9202	Tang. Diſt. cleared of Refr. 56°. 19′	10.1762
Prop. Log. of 58. 50 or firſt Arc	20.48;6	Prop. Log. of 35′. 50″ or ſecond Arc	20.6891

Second Arc 36. 50
Par. in Diſt. 22. 0

Table IV. Parallax in Altitude 26 gives 4
    Parallax in Diſtance 22 . . . 3

Second Correction of Parallax 1

Diſtance cleared of Refraction 56. 18. 45
Parallax in Diſtance . . . . — 22. 0

                                   55. 56. 45
Second Correction of Parallax . . . . . . + 1

Diſtance cleared of Refraction and Parallax . . 55. 56. 46

REMARKS.

I. In computing the Effect of Refraction, three Places of Figures, besides the Index, will generally be sufficient for Table I. but for finding the Effect of Parallax, the Sines &c. ought to be taken to four Places of Figures, besides the Index.

II. Sherwin's Logarithms are the most convenient and exact for these and other Calculations; but if a Set of Logarithms be used, having no Cosecants, they are easily found, by taking the Complement of the logarithmic Sine to 20.0000. Thus, to find the Cosecant of 48°. 19′, subtract its logarithmic Sine 9.8732 from 20.0000, the Remainder 10.1268 is the Cosecant required, as above in Example III.

III. If the Index of the proportional Logarithm of Arc first or second for Parallax come out 19, so that 20 cannot be thrown off, add 0.3010, or the Logarithm of 2 to the Sum of the Logarithms, and then abating 20 from the Index, find what Number it answers to in the Table of proportional Logarithms; which doubled, gives Arc the first or second.

IV. If the Moon's Distance was taken from the Sun instead of a Star, for Star read Sun in the preceding Rules.

SUPPLEMENTAL

TABLES

TO BE USED FOR CORRECTING

THE II^D AND III^D TABLES

FOR

REFRACTION,

AND FOR FINDING THE EFFECT OF THE

SUN'S PARÀLLAX,

WHERE IT IS REQUIRED TO HAVE

THE RESULT TRUE TO A SECOND.

BY MR. LYONS.

Table I. Supplemental,

Shewing what Number of Seconds is to be subtracted from the Number in Table II. on account of the greater Altitude of the Moon or Star, when under 30°.

Distance	Greater Altitude of the Moon or Star.												
	5°	6°	7°	8°	9°	10°	11°	12°	13°	14°	15°	16°	17°
°	″	″	″	″	″	″	″	″	″	″	″	″	″
10	28	21	16	13	10	8	7	6	5	4	4	3	3
11	26	19	15	12	9	8	6	5	5	4	4	3	3
12	23	17	14	11	8	7	6	5	4	3	3	3	3
13	22	16	13	10	8	6	6	5	4	3	3	3	3
14	20	14	12	9	7	6	5	4	4	3	3	3	2
15	19	13	11	9	7	6	5	4	3	3	3	3	2
16	17	13	10	8	6	5	5	4	3	3	3	3	2
17	16	12	9	8	6	5	4	4	3	3	3	3	2
18	15	11	9	7	5	4	4	3	3	2	2	2	2
19	14	10	8	7	5	4	3	3	3	2	2	2	2
20	14	10	8	6	5	4	3	3	3	2	2	2	2
21	13	10	8	5	5	4	3	3	3	2	2	2	2
22	12	9	7	6	4	4	3	3	3	2	2	2	2
23	12	9	7	5	4	4	3	2	2	2	2	2	1
24	11	8	6	5	4	3	3	2	2	2	1	1	1
25	11	8	6	5	4	3	3	2	2	2	1	1	1
26	10	7	6	5	4	3	3	2	2	2	1	1	1
27	10	7	6	5	4	3	3	2	2	2	1	1	1
28	9	7	5	4	3	3	2	2	2	1	1	1	1
29	9	7	5	4	3	2	2	2	2	1	1	1	1
30	9	6	5	4	3	3	2	2	2	1	1	1	1
35	7	5	4	3	3	2	2	2	1	1	1	1	1
40	6	4	3	3	2	2	2	2	1	1	1	1	1
45	5	4	3	2	2	1	2	1	1	1	1	1	1
50	4	3	2	2	1	1	1	1	1	1	1	1	0
55	3	2	2	2	1	1	1	1	1	0	0	0	0
120 / 60	3	2	2	1	1	1	1	1	1	0	0	0	0
110 / 70	2	1	1	1	1	0	1	0	0	0	0	0	0
100 / 80	1	1	0	0	0	0	0	0	0	0	0	0	0
90 / 90	0	0	0	0	0	0	0	0	0	0	0	0	0

TABLE I. Supplemental, continued, [31]

Shewing what Number of Seconds is to be subtracted from the Number in Table II. on account of the greater Altitude of the Moon or Star, when under 30°.

Distance	Distance	Greater Altitude of the Moon or Star.												
		18°	19°	20°	21°	22°	23°	24°	25°	26°	27°	28°	29°	30°
	°	"	"	"	"	"	"	"	"	"	"	"	"	"
	10	3	2	2	2	2	2	1	1	1	1	1	1	1
	11	3	2	2	2	2	2	1	1	1	1	1	1	1
	12	3	2	2	2	2	2	1	1	1	1	1	1	1
	13	2	2	2	2	2	2	1	1	1	1	1	1	1
	14	2	1	1	1	1	1	1	1	1	1	1	1	1
	15	2	1	1	1	1	1	1	1	1	1	1	1	1
	16	2	1	1	1	1	1	1	1	1	1	1	1	1
	17	2	1	1	1	1	1	1	1	1	1	1	1	1
	18	1	1	1	1	1	1	1	1	0	0	0	0	0
	19	1	1	1	1	1	1	1	1	0	0	0	0	0
	20	1	1	1	1	1	1	1	0	0	0	0	0	0
	21	1	1	1	1	1	1	1	0	0	0	0	0	0
	22	1	1	1	1	1	1	1	0	0	0	0	0	0
	23	1	1	1	1	1	1	1	0	0	0	0	0	0
	24	1	1	1	1	1	1	1	0	0	0	0	0	0
	25	1	1	1	1	1	1	1	0	0	0	0	0	0
	26	1	1	1	1	1	1	0	0	0	0	0	0	0
	27	1	1	1	1	1	0	0	0	0	0	0	0	0
	28	1	1	1	1	0	0	0	0	0	0	0	0	0
	29	1	1	1	1	0	0	0	0	0	0	0	0	0
	30	1	1	1	1	0	0	0	0	0	0	0	0	0
Distance °	35	1	0	0	0	0	0	0	0	0	0	0	0	0
	40	1	0	0	0	0	0	0	0	0	0	0	0	0
	45	0	0	0	0	0	0	0	0	0	0	0	0	0
	50	0	0	0	0	0	0	0	0	0	0	0	0	0
	55	0	0	0	0	0	0	0	0	0	0	0	0	0
120	60	0	0	0	0	0	0	0	0	0	0	0	0	0
110	70	0	0	0	0	0	0	0	0	0	0	0	0	0
100	80	0	0	0	0	0	0	0	0	0	0	0	0	0
90	90	0	0	0	0	0	0	0	0	0	0	0	0	0

TABLE II. Supplemental,

Shewing what Number of Seconds is to be added to the Number in Table II. standing under 10 Degrees, when the lesser Altitude is above 10 Degrees.

Distance.	Lesser Altitude of the Moon or Star.									
	11	12	13	14	15	16	17	18	19	20
°	"	"	"	"	"	"	"	"	"	"
10	1	2	3	4	5	5	5	6	6	6
11	1	2	3	4	4	5	5	5	6	6
12	1	2	3	4	4	4	4	5	5	5
13	1	2	2	3	3	4	4	4	5	5
14	1	2	2	3	3	4	4	4	4	4
15	1	1	2	3	3	3	4	4	4	4
16	1	1	2	2	3	3	3	3	4	4
17	1	1	2	2	3	3	3	3	4	4
18	1	1	2	2	2	3	3	3	3	3
19	1	1	2	2	2	3	3	3	3	3
20	1	1	2	2	2	2	3	3	3	3
21	1	1	2	2	2	2	2	3	3	3
22	1	1	1	2	2	2	2	2	3	3
23	1	1	1	2	2	2	2	2	3	3
24	1	1	1	2	2	2	2	2	2	2
25	0	1	1	1	2	2	2	2	2	2
26	0	1	1	1	2	2	2	2	2	2
27	0	1	1	1	2	2	2	2	2	2
28	0	1	1	1	2	2	2	2	2	2
29	0	1	1	1	1	2	2	2	2	2
30	0	1	1	1	1	2	2	2	2	2
35	0	1	1	1	1	1	1	1	1	1
40	0	0	1	1	1	1	1	1	1	1
45	0	0	1	1	1	1	1	1	1	1
50	0	0	0	1	1	1	1	1	1	1
55	0	0	0	0	1	1	1	1	1	1
60	0	0	0	0	0	1	1	1	1	1
70	0	0	0	0	0	0	0	0	0	0
80	0	0	0	0	0	0	0	0	0	0
90	0	0	0	0	0	0	0	0	0	0

TABLE II. Supplemental, continued, [33]

Shewing what Number of Seconds is to be added to the Number in Table II. standing under 10 Degrees, when the lesser Altitude is above 10 Degrees.

Distance	Lesser Altitude of the Moon or Star.									
°	21	22	23	24	25	26	27	28	29	30
°	"	"	"	"	"	"	"	"	"	"
10	6	7	7	7	7	7	7	7	7	7
11	6	6	6	6	6	6	6	7	7	7
12	5	5	6	5	6	6	6	6	6	6
13	5	5	5	5	5	5	5	6	6	6
14	4	5	5	5	5	5	5	5	5	5
15	4	4	4	4	4	4	5	5	5	5
16	4	4	4	4	4	4	4	5	5	5
17	4	4	4	4	4	4	4	4	4	4
18	3	3	4	4	4	4	4	4	4	4
19	3	3	3	3	3	3	3	4	4	4
20	3	3	3	3	3	3	3	3	3	3
21	3	3	3	3	3	3	3	3	3	3
22	3	3	3	3	3	3	3	3	3	3
23	3	3	3	3	3	3	3	3	3	3
24	2	3	3	3	3	3	3	3	3	3
25	2	2	2	2	2	2	3	3	3	3
26	2	2	2	2	2	2	3	3	3	3
27	2	2	2	2	2	2	2	3	3	3
28	2	2	2	1	2	2	2	2	2	2
29	2	2	2	2	2	2	2	2	2	2
30	2	2	2	2	2	2	2	2	2	2
35	1	2	2	2	2	2	2	2	2	2
40	1	1	1	1	1	1	1	2	2	2
45	1	1	1	1	1	1	1	1	1	1
50	1	1	1	1	1	1	1	1	1	1
55	1	1	1	1	1	1	1	1	1	1
66	1	1	1	1	1	1	1	1	1	1
70	0	0	0	0	0	0	0	0	0	0
80	0	0	0	0	0	0	0	0	0	0
90	0	0	0	0	0	0	0	0	0	0

E

TABLE III. Supplemental.

This Table, jointly with the following, is for finding the Correction of Table III.

This Table gives the Number for entering the first upright Column of the following Table.

Alt.	50	51	52	53	54	55	56	57	58	59	60	61
°	"											
50	0	"										
51	0	0	"									
52	0,1	0	0	"								
53	0,1	0,1	0	0	"							
54	0,2	0,1	0,1	0	0	"						
55	0,3	0,2	0,2	0,1	0,1	0	"					
56	0,4	0,3	0,3	0,2	0,1	0,1	0	"				
57	0,5	0,4	0,4	0,3	0,2	0,1	0,1	0	"			
58	0,6	0,5	0,4	0,4	0,3	0,2	0,1	0,1	0	"		
59	0,8	0,6	0,5	0,4	0,3	0,2	0,2	0,1	0,1	0	"	
60	0,9	0,7	0,6	0,5	0,3	0,2	0,2	0,1	0,1	0	0	"
61	1,0	0,9	0,7	0,6	0,4	0,3	0,2	0,2	0,2	0,1	0,1	0
62	1,2	1,0	0,8	0,6	0,5	0,3	0,2	0,2	0,2	0,1	0,1	0
63	1,3	1,1	0,9	0,7	0,6	0,4	0,3	0,3	0,2	0,1	0,1	0,1
64	1,5	1,3	1,1	0,9	0,7	0,5	0,4	0,3	0,3	0,2	0,1	0,1
65	1,6	1,4	1,2	1,0	0,8	0,6	0,5	0,4	0,3	0,2	0,1	0,1
66	1,8	1,6	1,4	1,1	0,9	0,7	0,6	0,5	0,3	0,2	0,1	0,1
67	1,9	1,7	1,5	1,2	1,0	0,8	0,7	0,6	0,4	0,3	0,2	0,2
68	2,1	1,9	1,6	1,4	1,1	0,9	0,8	0,7	0,5	0,4	0,3	0,2
69	2,2	2,0	1,7	1,5	1,2	1,0	0,9	0,7	0,6	0,4	0,3	0,3
70	2,4	2,1	1,8	1,6	1,3	1,1	1,0	0,8	0,7	0,5	0,4	0,3
71	2,5	2,2	2,0	1,7	1,5	1,2	1,1	0,9	0,8	0,6	0,5	0,4
72	2,7	2,4	2,1	1,9	1,6	1,3	1,1	1,0	0,8	0,7	0,6	0,4
73	2,8	2,5	2,2	2,0	1,7	1,4	1,2	1,1	0,9	0,8	0,6	0,5
74	3,0	2,7	2,4	2,1	1,8	1,5	1,3	1,1	1,0	0,8	0,6	0,5
75	3,1	2,8	2,5	2,2	1,9	1,6	1,4	1,2	1,1	0,9	0,7	0,6
76	3,2	2,9	2,6	2,3	2,0	1,7	1,5	1,3	1,2	1,0	0,8	0,7
77	3,3	3,0	2,7	2,4	2,1	1,8	1,6	1,3	1,2	1,0	0,9	0,7
78	3,4	3,1	2,8	2,4	2,1	1,8	1,6	1,4	1,3	1,1	0,9	0,8
79	3,5	3,2	2,9	2,5	2,2	1,9	1,7	1,5	1,3	1,1	0,9	0,8
80	3,6	3,3	2,9	2,6	2,3	2,0	1,8	1,6	1,4	1,2	1,0	0,8
81	3,7	3,4	2,9	2,6	2,3	2,0	1,8	1,6	1,4	1,2	1,0	0,9
82	3,8	3,5	3,0	2,7	2,4	2,1	1,9	1,6	1,4	1,3	1,1	0,9
83	3,9	3,5	3,1	2,7	2,4	2,1	1,9	1,6	1,4	1,3	1,1	1,0
84	4,0	3,5	3,2	2,8	2,5	2,2	2,0	1,7	1,5	1,4	1,2	1,0
85	4,0	3,6	3,2	2,8	2,5	2,2	2,0	1,8	1,5	1,4	1,2	1,0
90	4,1	3,7	3,3	2,9	2,6	2,3	2,1	1,9	1,6	1,4	1,2	1,1

TABLE III. Supplemental, continued.   [35]

This Table, jointly with the following, is for finding the Correction of Table III.

This Table gives the Number for entering the first upright Column of the following Table.

Alt.	62	63	64	65	66	67	68	69	70	75	80	85	90
0													
50													
51													
52													
53													
54													
55													
56													
57													
58													
59													
60													
61	"												
62	0	"											
63	0	0	"										
64	0	0	0	"									
65	0,1	0	0	0	"								
66	0,1	0	0	0	0	"							
67	0,1	0,1	0	0	0	0	"						
68	0,2	0,1	0	0	0	0	0	"					
69	0,2	0,2	0,1	0,1	0,1	0	0	0	"				
70	0,3	0,2	0,2	0,1	0,1	0,1	0	0	0	"			
71	0,3	0,3	0,2	0,1	0,1	0,1	0	0	0		"		
72	0,4	0,3	0,3	0,2	0,2	0,1	0,1	0	0	0		"	
73	0,4	0,4	0,3	0,2	0,2	0,1	0,1	0	0	0			"
74	0,5	0,4	0,3	0,3	0,3	0,2	0,2	0,1	0,1	0			
75	0,5	0,4	0,4	0,3	0,3	0,2	0,2	0,1	0,1	0			
76	0,6	0,5	0,4	0,3	0,3	0,2	0,2	0,1	0,1	0	0		
77	0,6	0,5	0,4	0,3	0,3	0,2	0,2	0,1	0,1	0	0		
78	0,7	0,6	0,5	0,4	0,3	0,3	0,2	0,1	0,1	0	0		
79	0,7	0,6	0,5	0,4	0,3	0,3	0,2	0,1	0,1	0	0		
80	0,7	0,6	0,5	0,4	0,3	0,3	0,2	0,1	0,1	0			
81	0,7	0,6	0,5	0,4	0,3	0,3	0,2	0,1	0,1	0	0		
82	0,8	0,7	0,6	0,4	0,3	0,3	0,2	0,1	0,1	0	0		
83	0,8	0,7	0,6	0,5	0,4	0,4	0,3	0,2	0,2	0,1	0	0	
84	0,8	0,7	0,6	0,5	0,4	0,4	0,3	0,2	0,2	0,1	0	0	
85	0,8	0,7	0,6	0,5	0,4	0,4	0,3	0,2	0,2	0,1	0	0	
90	0,9	0,8	0,7	0,6	0,5	0,5	0,4	0,3	0,2	0,1	0	0	0

TABLE IV. Supplemental,

For finding the Correction to be added to Table III. where both Altitudes are above 50 Degrees.

N° found by preceding Table	Distance																			
	10	11	12	13	14	15	16	17	18	19	20	21	22	23	24	25	26	27	28	29
0,1	0	0	0	0	0	0	0	0	0	0	0	0	0	0	0	0	0	0	0	0
0,2	1	1	1	1	1	1	1	1	1	1	1	1	1	0	0	0	0	0	0	0
0,3	2	2	1	1	1	1	1	1	1	1	1	1	1	1	1	1	1	1	1	1
0,4	2	2	2	2	2	2	1	1	1	1	1	1	1	1	1	1	1	1	1	1
0,5	3	3	2	2	2	2	2	2	2	2	1	1	1	1	1	1	1	1	1	1
0,6	3	3	3	3	2	2	2	2	2	2	2	2	2	1	1	1	1	1	1	1
0,7	4	4	3	3	3	3	3	2	2	2	2	2	2	2	2	2	2	1	1	1
0,8	5	4	4	4	3	3	3	3	3	2	2	2	2	2	2	2	2	2	2	2
0,9	5	5	4	4	4	3	3	3	3	3	2	2	2	2	2	2	2	2	2	2
1,0	6	5	5	4	4	4	4	3	3	3	3	3	3	2	2	2	2	2	2	2
1,1	6	6	5	5	5	4	4	4	4	3	3	3	3	3	3	2	2	2	2	2
1,2	-	6	6	5	5	5	4	4	4	4	3	3	3	3	3	3	3	3	3	2
1,3	-	-	6	6	5	5	5	4	4	4	4	4	3	3	3	3	3	3	3	3
1,4	-	-	6	6	5	5	5	5	4	4	4	4	4	3	3	3	3	3	3	3
1,5	-	-	-	7	6	6	5	5	5	5	4	4	4	4	4	4	3	3	3	3
1,6	-	-	-	-	6	6	5	5	5	5	5	4	4	4	4	4	4	4	3	3
1,7	-	-	-	-	7	6	6	5	5	5	5	5	4	4	4	4	4	4	4	3
1,8	-	-	-	-	7	6	6	6	6	5	5	5	5	4	4	4	4	4	4	4
1,9	-	-	-	-	-	7	6	6	6	6	5	5	5	5	4	4	4	4	4	4
2,0	-	-	-	-	-	7	7	6	6	6	6	5	5	5	5	4	4	4	4	4
2,1	-	-	-	-	-	-	7	7	6	6	6	6	5	5	5	5	5	4	4	4
2,2	-	-	-	-	-	-	-	7	7	6	6	6	6	5	5	5	5	5	5	5
2,3	-	-	-	-	-	-	-	7	7	6	6	6	6	5	5	5	5	5	5	5
2,4	-	-	-	-	-	-	-	-	7	7	6	6	6	6	6	5	5	5	5	5
2,5	-	-	-	-	-	-	-	-	-	7	7	7	6	6	6	6	5	5	5	5
2,6	-	-	-	-	-	-	-	-	-	-	8	7	7	7	6	6	6	6	6	5
2,7	-	-	-	-	-	-	-	-	-	-	8	7	7	7	6	6	6	6	6	6
2,8	-	-	-	-	-	-	-	-	-	-	-	7	7	7	7	6	6	6	6	6
2,9	-	-	-	-	-	-	-	-	-	-	-	8	7	7	7	7	6	6	6	6
3,0	-	-	-	-	-	-	-	-	-	-	-	8	7	7	7	7	6	6	6	6
3,1	-	-	-	-	-	-	-	-	-	-	-	-	8	7	7	7	7	7	7	6
3,2	-	-	-	-	-	-	-	-	-	-	-	-	-	8	7	7	7	7	7	7
3,3	-	-	-	-	-	-	-	-	-	-	-	-	-	-	7	7	7	7	7	7
3,4	-	-	-	-	-	-	-	-	-	-	-	-	-	-	-	7	7	7	7	7
3,5	-	-	-	-	-	-	-	-	-	-	-	-	-	-	-	-	7	7	7	7
3,6	-	-	-	-	-	-	-	-	-	-	-	-	-	-	-	-	-	-	-	7
3,7	-	-	-	-	-	-	-	-	-	-	-	-	-	-	-	-	-	-	-	-
3,8	-	-	-	-	-	-	-	-	-	-	-	-	-	-	-	-	-	-	-	-
3,9	-	-	-	-	-	-	-	-	-	-	-	-	-	-	-	-	-	-	-	-
4,0	-	-	-	-	-	-	-	-	-	-	-	-	-	-	-	-	-	-	-	-

TABLE IV. Supplemental, continued, [37]

For finding the Correction to be added to Table III. where both Altitudes are above 50 Degrees.

N° found by preceding Table	Distance.																		
	30	31	32	33	34	35	36	37	38	39	40	41	42	43	44	45	50	55	60 & above
″	″	″	″	″	″	″	″	″	″	″	″	″	″	″	″	″	″	″	″
0,1	0	0	0	0	0	0	0	0	0	0	0	0	0	0	0	0	0	0	0
0,2	0	0	0	0	0	0	0	0	0	0	0	0	0	0	0	0	0	0	0
0,3	1	1	1	1	1	1	1	1	0	0	0	0	0	0	0	0	0	0	0
0,4	1	1	1	1	1	1	1	1	1	1	1	1	1	1	1	0	0	0	0
0,5	1	1	1	1	1	1	1	1	1	1	1	1	1	1	1	1	1	1	0
0,6	1	1	1	1	1	1	1	1	1	1	1	1	1	1	1	1	1	1	1
0,7	1	1	1	1	1	1	1	1	1	1	1	1	1	1	1	1	1	1	1
0,8	2	1	2	1	1	1	1	1	1	1	1	1	1	1	1	1	1	1	1
0,9	2	2	2	2	2	2	2	1	1	1	1	1	1	1	1	1	1	1	1
1,0	2	2	2	2	2	2	2	2	2	2	2	1	1	1	1	1	1	1	1
1,1	2	2	2	2	2	2	2	2	2	2	2	2	2	2	1	1	1	1	1
1,2	2	2	2	2	2	2	2	2	2	2	2	2	2	2	2	2	1	1	1
1,3	3	3	2	2	2	2	2	2	2	2	2	2	2	2	2	2	2	2	1
1,4	3	3	3	3	3	2	2	2	2	2	2	2	2	2	2	2	2	2	2
1,5	3	3	3	3	3	3	2	2	2	2	2	2	2	2	2	2	2	2	2
1,6	3	3	3	3	3	3	3	3	3	3	3	2	2	2	2	2	2	2	2
1,7	3	3	3	3	3	3	3	3	3	3	3	3	3	2	2	2	2	2	2
1,8	4	3	3	3	3	3	3	3	3	3	3	3	3	3	3	2	2	2	2
1,9	4	4	3	3	3	3	3	3	3	3	3	3	3	3	3	2	2	2	2
2,0	4	4	4	4	4	3	3	3	3	3	3	3	3	3	3	3	3	2	2
2,1	4	4	4	4	4	4	4	3	3	3	3	3	3	3	3	3	3	2	2
2,2	4	4	4	4	4	4	4	4	4	3	3	3	3	3	3	3	3	3	2
2,3	5	4	4	4	4	4	4	4	4	4	4	3	3	3	3	3	3	3	3
2,4	5	5	5	4	4	4	4	4	4	4	4	4	3	3	3	3	3	3	3
2,5	5	5	5	5	4	4	4	4	4	4	4	4	4	4	4	3	3	3	3
2,6	5	5	5	5	5	5	5	4	4	4	4	4	4	4	4	4	3	3	3
2,7	5	5	5	5	5	5	5	5	4	4	4	4	4	4	4	4	3	3	3
2,8	6	5	5	5	5	5	5	5	4	4	4	4	4	4	4	4	3	3	3
2,9	6	6	5	5	5	5	5	5	5	5	4	4	4	4	4	4	4	3	3
3,0	6	6	6	6	5	5	5	5	5	5	5	5	4	4	4	4	4	4	4
3,1	6	6	6	6	6	5	5	5	5	5	5	5	5	4	4	4	4		
3,2	6	6	6	6	6	6	6	5	5	5	5	5	5	5	5	4	4		
3,3	7	7	6	6	6	6	6	6	5	5	5	5	5	5	5	4	4		
3,4	7	7	6	6	6	6	6	6	6	5	5	5	5	5	5	4			
3,5	7	7	7	6	6	6	6	6	6	6	5	5	5	5	5	4			
3,6	7	7	7	7	6	6	6	6	6	6	6	5	5	5	5	5			
3,7	7	7	7	7	7	7	6	6	6	6	6	6	6	5	5	5			
3,8		7	7	7	7	7	6	6	6	6	6	6	6	5	5				
3,9			7	7	7	7	6	6	6	6	6	6	6	5					
4,0				7	7		6	6	6	6	6	6	6						
4,1					7	7	7	6	6	6	6	6	6						

TABLE V. Supplemental.

For the Effect of the Sun's Parallax.

Apparent Distance of the Sun and Moon.													
Subtract from apparent Distance.													
Alt. ☽	30	35	40	45	50	55	60	65	70	75	80	85	90
°	′	″	″	″	″	″	″	″	″	″	″	″	″
5	2	2	1	1	1	1	1	1	1	1	1	1	1
10	3	3	2	2	2	2	2	2	2	2	2	2	2
15	5	4	4	3	3	3	3	3	2	2	2	2	2
20	6	5	5	4	4	4	3	3	3	3	3	3	3
25	7	6	6	5	5	5	4	4	4	4	4	4	4
30	9	8	7	6	6	5	5	5	5	4	4	4	4
35	10	9	8	7	7	6	6	6	5	5	5	5	5
40	11	10	9	8	7	7	6	6	6	6	6	6	6
45	12	11	10	9	8	8	7	7	7	6	6	6	6
50	13	12	10	10	9	8	8	7	7	7	7	7	7
55	14	13	11	10	9	9	8	8	8	8	7	7	7
60	15	13	12	11	10	9	9	8	8	8	8	8	8
65	16	14	12	11	10	10	9	9	8	8	9	8	8
70	17	15	13	12	11	10	10	9	9	9	9	8	8
75	17	15	13	12	11	10	10	9	9	9	9	9	8
80	17	15	13	12	11	11	10	10	9	9	9	9	9
85	18	16	14	12	11	11	10	10	9	9	9	9	9
90	18	16	14	12	11	11	10	10	9	9	9	9	9
							120	115	110	105	100	95	90

App. Dist. of the Sun and Moon.

Subtract from app. Distance.

TABLE VI. Supplemental.

For the Effect of the Sun's Parallax.

	Apparent Distance of the Sun and Moon.												
	Add to apparent Distance.												
Alt. ⊙	30	35	40	45	50	55	60	65	70	75	80	85	90
°	″	″	″	″	″	″	″	″	″	″	″	″	″
5	1	1	1	1	1	0	0	0	0	0	0	0	0
10	3	2	2	2	1	1	1	1	1	0	0	0	0
15	4	3	3	2	2	2	1	1	1	0	0	0	0
20	5	4	4	3	2	2	2	1	1	1	0	0	0
25	6	5	4	4	3	2	2	2	1	1	1	0	0
30	8	6	5	4	4	3	2	2	2	1	1	0	0
35	9	7	6	5	4	3	3	2	2	1	1	0	0
40	10	8	7	6	5	4	3	3	2	2	1	0	0
45	11	9	7	6	5	4	4	3	2	2	1	1	0
50	12	10	8	7	6	5	4	3	2	2	1	1	0
55	13	10	8	7	6	5	4	3	3	2	1	1	0
60	13	11	9	8	6	5	4	4	3	2	1	1	0
65	14	11	9	8	7	6	5	4	3	2	1	1	0
70	14	12	10	8	7	6	5	4	3	2	1	1	0
75	15	12	10	8	7	6	5	4	3	2	2	1	0
80	15	13	10	9	7	6	5	4	3	2	2	1	0
85	15	13	10	9	7	6	5	4	3	2	2	1	0
90	15	13	11	9	7	6	5	4	3	2	2	1	0
							120	115	110	105	100	95	90
							App. Dist. of the Sun and Moon.						
							Subtract from app. Distance.						

EXPLICATION

OF THE USE OF THE

SUPPLEMENTAL TABLES,

THESE Tables are only neceffary to be ufed where the utmoft Accuracy is required; and therefore may very well be omitted in common Practice, fince the Effect of them will never amount to 10″ (and generally much lefs) if the greater of the two Altitudes of the Moon and Star be 10ᵈ or above, as it can fcarcely ever be lefs. Their Titles almoft fufficiently explain their Ufe: neverthelefs, it may be proper to add the following Directions concerning them.

Tables I. and II. Supplemental, are to be both ufed in cor-recting Table II. of Refraction. Enter Table I. Supplemen-tal with greater Altitude of the Moon or Star at Top; and Diftance on the Side, the correfponding Number of Seconds is to be fubftracted from that taken out of Table II. of Re-fraction. Then enter Table II. Supplemental with leffer Al-titude of the Moon or Star at Top, and Diftance on the Side, the correfponding Number of Seconds added to Number in Table II. of Refraction, firft already corrected for Table I. Supplemental, gives the Number in Table II. of Refraction corrected, which muft be applied as before.

Note. That when the utmoft Accuracy is required, Tables I. and II. of Refraction are to be ufed together with the two firft fupplemental Tables, if one or both Altitudes are under 50°, as well in the Cafes falling to the right Hand of the black waving Line as in the reft of the Table; and Table III. of Refraction is only to be ufed, where both Altitudes are above 50°. In this Cafe, and this Cafe only, Tables III. and IV. Supplemental are to be ufed for correcting Table III. of Refraction. Enter Table III. Supplemental with leffer Altitude

titude of the Moon or Star at the Top, and greater Altitude on the Side, and take out the corresponding Number; with which enter Table IV. Supplemental on the Side, and entering the same Table with the Distance on the Top, the corresponding Number of Seconds is the Correction to be added to Table III. of Refraction.

The two last Tables, or V. and VI. Supplemental, serve for correcting the observed Distance of the Moon from the Sun, on account of the Sun's Parallax; their joint Effect cannot exceed 9″. Enter Table V. Supplemental with the Moon's Altitude on the Side, and the Distance at the Top; and enter Table VI. Supplemental with the Sun's Altitude on the Side, and Distance at the Top. The two Numbers so taken out, applied with their proper Signs respectively, according to the Directions indicated by the Tables, to the Distance already corrected by the preceding Tables and Rules, give the Distance further corrected on account of the Sun's Parallax.

Here follow the four Examples wrought before, according to the four principal Tables, corrected by the supplemental Tables.

EXAMPLE I. corrected.

The greater Altitude, namely that of the Star, being 24°. 48′, and the Distance 51½°, the Correction of Table II. Supplemental is 0; the lesser Altitude, namely of the Moon, being 12°. 30′, and the Distance 51½°, Table II. Supplemental also gives 0; so that the Number found by Table II. of Refraction, and consequently the Effect of Refraction, as found before, appears to be exact, without needing any further Correction.

Suppose now, that, instead of a Star, it had been the Sun, from which this Distance of the Moon was taken. Entering Table V. Supplemental with the Moon's Altitude 12½° on the Side, and Distance 51½° at the Top, the corresponding Number of Seconds is 2″, to be subtracted. In like Manner entering Table VI. with the Sun's Altitude 24°. 48′ on the Side, and Distance 51½° at Top, the Number of Seconds comes out 3″, to be added. Therefore 51°. 9′. 51″ — 2″ + 3″ = 51°. 9′. 52″, the reduced Distance correct.

F

Example II. corrected.

The greater Altitude, namely that of the Moon, being 27½°, and the Distance 102½°, Table I. Supplemental gives 0; the lesser Altitude, namely that of the Star, being 15°. 25′, and the Distance as before 102½°; Table II. also gives 0; whence the Effect of Refraction found before is exact.

Suppose now, that this had been the Moon's Distance from the Sun, instead of a Star, to correct the Distance further for the Effect of the Sun's Parallax, entering Table V. with 28°. 19′, the Moon's Altitude corrected both for Refraction and Parallax, and 102°. 11′, the Distance corrected, you find 4″, to be subtracted. Entering Table VI. Supplemental with the Sun's Altitude 15°. 22′, and Distance 102°. 11′, you find 0″; whence 102°. 11′. 11″ — 4″ = 102°. 11′. 7″, the Distance of the Moon from the Sun reduced or finally corrected.

Example III. corrected.

One of the Altitudes, namely that of the Moon being under 50°. This Case, though falling to the right-hand Side of the black waving Line, must not be computed by Table III. but by Tables I. and II. of Refraction, corrected by Tables I. and II. Supplemental; because the utmost Accuracy is supposed to be required.

Table I. gives 0641 + 2 — 6 = 0637, to which prefix the Index 2, it is . . . . } 2.0637
Cosecant Distance 33°15′ 10.2610

Logarithm of 211 . . . . 12.3247

The Number in Table II. in the Column intituled 10° and above, to Distance 33° being 174″, and to Distance 34°, being 167″, to 33°. 14′, there will answer 172″; but this must be corrected by Tables I. and II. Supplemental.

The greater Altitude being above 30°, Table I. Supplemental gives 0; the lesser Altitude being above 30°, and the Distance being 33°, Table II. gives 2″, to be added to 172″, makes 174″, to be subtracted from 211″, the Remainder 37″ is the Effect of Refraction to be added to the observed Distance 33°. 15′. 0″ gives the Distance cleared of Refraction 33°. 15′. 37″, or 3″ greater than found before by the applying Table III. only. The Calculation of the Effect of
Parallax

Parallax will not be altered hereby, so that the reduced Distance will come out 3″ greater than before, or 33°. 16′. 32″.

Suppose now the Distance was that of the Moon from the Sun, and not from a Star, to find the Effect of the Sun's Parallax, the Moon's Altitude corrected for Refraction and Parallax being 64°. 53′, and the Distance above corrected 33°. 16′, Table V. Supplemental gives 15″, to be subtracted; and the Sun's Altitude corrected being 48°. 19′, Table VI. Supplemental gives 10″, to be added. Therefore 33°. 16′. 32″ − 15″ + 10″ = 33°. 16′. 27″, the reduced or correct Distance of the Moon from the Sun.

Example IV. corrected.

Table III. Supplemental answering to the Altitude 65° and 53°, gives 1″,0; with which entering Table IV. Supplemental on the Side, and with the Distance 56° at the Top, there will be found 1″, to be added to 61″, the Number found by Table III. or it will come to the same thing, if it be added to the Distance above cleared of Refraction and Parallax, viz. 55°. 56′. 46″; whence the Distance further corrected will be 55°. 56′. 47″.

INVESTIGATION

OF THE

T A B L E S

A N D

R U L E S

FOR FINDING THE EFFECT OF

R E F R A C T I O N

A N D

P A R A L L A X

UPON THE

MOON's DISTANCE FROM A STAR.

LET Z be the Zenith, M the Moon, its Alt. $= \mu$, N the Star, its Altitude $= \nu$, Sine $\mu = M$, Cofine $\mu = m$, Sine $\nu = N$, Cofine $\nu = n$, Diftance M N $= \delta$, its Sine $= D$, and Cofine $= d$, Radius $= 1$. Putting μ to exprefs the Refraction in Altitude M m at the Altitude μ, and ν the Refraction in Altitude N n at the Altitude ν, and drawing the Arches N ι, N r perpendicular to the true Diftance μn, the Diftance is contracted by Refraction, by the

Quantity

Quantity $m\dot{i} + m\dot{r} = N\dot{n} \times Cof.\, n + M\, m \times Cof.\, m = \dot{i}$

$\times \dfrac{M - dN}{D\, n} + \mu \times \dfrac{N - dM}{D\, m} = \dfrac{1}{D} \times \overline{\dfrac{M\dot{i}}{n} + \dfrac{N\mu}{m}} - \dfrac{d}{D}$

$\times \overline{\dfrac{N\dot{i}}{n} + \dfrac{M\mu}{m}}.$

The Logarithms of $\dfrac{M\dot{i}}{n} + \dfrac{N\mu}{m}$ are contained in Table I. to which the logarithmic Cofecant of the Diftance, or the Logarithm of $\dfrac{1}{D}$ being added, the Sum is the Logarithm of the Quantity $\dfrac{1}{D} \times \overline{\dfrac{M\dot{i}}{n} + \dfrac{N\mu}{m}}$, or the firſt Part of the Formula above.

As the greater of the two Altitudes (fuppofe μ) can fcarcely be lefs than 10°, $\dfrac{M\mu}{m}$ may be confidered as a conſtant Quantity $= 57''$, the Refraction at the Altitude of 45°, which put $= \epsilon$; for, according to Dr. Bradley's Rule, $\mu = 57''$ $\times$ Cotang. $\mu + 3\mu = 57'' \times \dfrac{m}{M}$ nearly, when μ is 10° or more, and confequently $\dfrac{M\mu}{m} = 57'' = \epsilon$, whence the fecond Part of the Formula $\dfrac{d}{D} \times \overline{\dfrac{N\dot{i}}{n} + \dfrac{M\mu}{m}} = \dfrac{d}{D} \times \overline{\dfrac{N\dot{i}}{n} + \epsilon}$ very nearly, $\dot{r}$ being taken as the leſſer Altitude, the Values of which Expreſſion are contained in Table II.

Suppoſing the Refraction in Altitude to be accurately as the Tangents of the Zenith Diſtances, as they are very nearly for Altitudes above 10°, $\mu = \dfrac{\epsilon m}{M}$ and $\dot{i} = \dfrac{\epsilon n}{N}$, which ſubſtituted in the general Formula, it becomes $\dfrac{1}{D} \times \overline{\dfrac{\epsilon M}{N} + \dfrac{\epsilon N}{M}} - \dfrac{d}{D} \times 2\epsilon$, and ſubſtituting for the Cotang. $\dfrac{d}{D}$ it is equal $\dfrac{1}{D} - t$, t being the Tangent of Half the Diſtance, or $\frac{1}{2}\,\partial$, the general Formula is reduced to the following Expreſſion, $\dfrac{\epsilon}{D} \times \overline{\dfrac{M}{N} + \dfrac{N}{M}} - 2 + 2\epsilon t = 2\epsilon t + \dfrac{\epsilon}{D} \times \overline{\dfrac{M - N|^2}{M N}}.$

If both Altitudes are above 50°, the Quantity $\frac{e}{D} \times \overline{\frac{M - N}{MN}}$ will never exceed 8″; and therefore the Effect of Refraction may be taken $= 2et$, the Values of which are contained in Table III.

The Cafe is the fame with refpect to all the Places falling to the right Hand of the black waving Line in Table I. which therefore will alfo be found at once by Table III.

When the utmoft Accuracy is required, fome fmall Corrections muft be made to Tables I, II, and III. of Refraction, thefe are contained in the four firft fupplemental Tables, and are readily to be taken out at Sight. The Foundation of them is as follows. μ being $= e \times$ Colang. $\mu + 3 \mu = e$ $\times \overline{\frac{m}{M} - \frac{3\mu}{M^2}}$, nearly $=$ (or for μ fubftituting its approximate Value $\frac{em}{M}$, $=$) $e \times \overline{\frac{m}{M} - \frac{3em}{M^2}}$, it is plain that $\frac{M\mu}{m} = e - \frac{3e^2}{M^2}$.

In like Manner $\frac{N e}{n} = e - \frac{3e^2}{N^2}$. Whence $\frac{d}{D} \times \overline{\frac{N e}{n} + \frac{M\mu}{m}}$, the fecond Part of the general Formula, may be taken for Altitudes above 10°, very accurately, to be $== \frac{d}{D}$ $\times 2e - \frac{3e^2}{M^2} - \frac{3e^2}{N^2}$. But the Numbers in Table II. ftanding in the laft Column, intituled 10° and above, are $= \frac{d}{D} \times 112″,5$. and the Expreffion juft found above is $= \frac{d}{D} \times 114″ - \frac{3e^2}{M^2} - \frac{3e^2}{N^2}$, which is greater than $\frac{d}{D} \times 112″,5$ by $\frac{d}{D} \times \overline{1″\frac{1}{2} - \frac{3e^2}{M^2} - \frac{3e^2}{N^2}}$. This Correction, therefore, muft be applied to the Number taken out of the laft Column of Table II. This may be refolved into two Parts, $\frac{d}{D} \times 1″\frac{1}{2} - \frac{3e^2}{N^2}$ and $- \frac{d}{D} \times \frac{3e^2}{M^2}$.

The firft Part is contained in the fecond fupplemental Table, the other Part in the firft fupplemental Table: Only when the greater Altitude is under 10°, the Correction $- \frac{d}{D} \times \frac{3e^2}{M^2}$ being not quite exact, the Correction in that

Cafe

Cafe was found from the Formula $- \dfrac{d}{D} \times \overline{57'' - \dfrac{M\,\dot{u}}{m}}$; for it is plain that this Quantity added to $\dfrac{d}{D} \times \overline{\dfrac{N\,\dot{r}}{n} + 57''}$, the Quantity ftanding in the laft Column of Table II. makes $\dfrac{d}{D} \times \dfrac{N\,\dot{r}}{n} + \dfrac{M\,\mu}{m}$ the fecond Part of the general Formula.

It has been fhewn above, that when both Altitudes are confiderable the Effect of Refraction $= 2\,\epsilon t + \dfrac{\epsilon}{D} \times \overline{\dfrac{M-N]^2}{MN}}$, the principal Part $2\,\epsilon t$ being contained in Table III. the other Part ferves as a Correction to it: the third fupplemental Table contains the Values of $\epsilon \times \overline{\dfrac{M-N]^2}{MN}}$, and the fourth fupplemental Table ferves to multiply this laft Quantity by $\dfrac{1}{D}$, or the Cofecant of the Diftance, in order to obtain the required Correction of Table III. of Refraction.

Inveftigation of the two Rules for finding the Effect of PARALLAX.

Let $h =$ horizontal Parallax; then $M\textbf{m} = h\textbf{m}$, and $M\,r = M\textbf{m} \times$ Cof. M $= h\textbf{m} \times \dfrac{N-d\,M}{D\textbf{m}} = \dfrac{N\,h}{D}$

$\dfrac{h\,d\,M}{D} =$ horizontal Parallax $\times$ Sine of the Star's Altitude $\times$ Cofec. Dift. $=$ horizontal Parallax $\times$ Sine of the Moon's Alt. $\times$ Cotang. Diftance.

The Effect of the Sun's Parallax might be found in the fame Manner; but being very fmall, is conveniently thrown into two fhort Tables, the Vth and VIth fupplemental ones.

Table IV. for Parallax contains the Product of the Verfefines of the Number of Minutes contained in the firft Column, and the Cotangent of the Numbers at the Top of the Table, reduced into Seconds.

The

The Difference of the two Numbers taken out of this Table expresses the Quantity of the second Correction of Parallax, delivered in the Preface to the British Mariner's Guide; for the Investigation of which, see Philosophical Transactions, Vol. LIV. p. 273. for the Year 1764.

N. B. Table IV. will be found useful, as a general Table, for many other Purposes, where the Fluxions of spherical Triangles are concerned; of which take one

EXAMPLE.

Let it be required to find the Deviation of a Star's Parallel of Declination from the fixed horizontal Wire of a Quadrant placed in the Meridian, at any small given Distance of the Star from the Meridian. Enter the Table with the Star's Distance from the nearest Pole of the Equator at Top, and the given Distance from the Meridian, expressed in Minutes of a great Circle on the Side (in the Column marked Parallaxes) and you will find the Deviation required. Suppose the Distance of the Star from the Pole to be 10°, and the Distance from the Meridian to be 30′ of an Arch of a great Circle, the Deviation will be found 45″.

PROBLEM.

Having given the Hypothenuse δ, and one Leg β, of a right-angled spherical Triangle, to find the Angle opposite to this Leg.

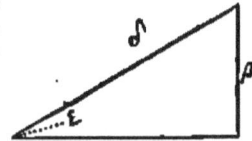

Let ϵ be the Angle of a right-angled rectilinear Triangle, whose Hypothenuse is δ, and one Side β, and in Table IV. find what Number of Seconds answers to β in the Column of Parallaxes, and ϵ among the Distances; ¼ of this Number added to the Angle ϵ in the rectilinear Triangle, will give the spherical Angle.

EXAMPLE.

Let $\beta = 1°$, $\delta = 2°$, and therefore $\epsilon = 30°$; the Number in Table IV. answering to 60′ and 30° is 54″, ¼ of which is 18″; whence the spherical Angle $= 30°. 0′. 18″$.

[This was communicated by Mr. LYONS.]

CORRECTION

CORRECTION

TO BE APPLIED TO THE

EFFECT of REFRACTION

Found by the above or any other Method,

On account of the Barometer and Thermometer.

THE Refractions in Altitude, and consequently the Effect of Refraction upon the Moon's Distance from a Star, varying with the Changes of the Temperature of the Air, indicated by the Barometer and Thermometer, it becomes necessary to pay a Regard to this Circumstance, when the utmost Accuracy is required, and therefore as often as the supplemental Tables are made use of.

The Table of Refractions in Altitude, p. 1. was adapted by Dr. Bradley to the Altitude 50° of Fahrenheit's Thermometer, and the Altitude 29,6 Inches of the Barometer; and it will answer equally to the Altitude 55 of the Thermometer, and 30 Inches of the Barometer, which is about its mean Altitude at the Level of the Sea.

When they are at any other Heights, to find what Correction must be made to the Effect of Refraction, already found by Tables I. and II. or Table III. with the supplemental Tables; say, As 400 is to the Difference of the Thermometer from 55°; so is the Effect of Refraction, before found, to its Correction required; to be subtracted from thence, if the Thermometer is higher than 55°; but to be added, if the Thermometer is lower.

Take the Difference between the Altitude of the Barometer and 30 Inches, and say, As 300 is to the said Difference, expressed in Tenths of an Inch; so is the Effect of Refraction corrected for the Thermometer, to the Correction required on account of the Barometer; which added to or subtracted from the Effect of Refraction corrected for the Thermometer, according

G

cording

cording as the Barometer is higher or lower than 30 Inches, gives the true Effect of Refraction corrected on account of both.

The common Barometer not being proper to be ufed at Sea, and the Changes of Refraction relative to this Inftrument being generally much lefs than thofe anfwering to the Changes of the Thermometer, efpecially near and between the Tropics, perhaps the Correction of the Effect of Refraction on account of the Barometer will generally be omitted, except the In-ftrument called the Marine Barometer fhall be found, or be improved, to be of fufficient Exactnefs for Ufe at Sea.

The Thermometer made ufe of fhould be of Fahrenheit's Scale; and if not kept always in a fhady Place in the open Air, fhould be brought out when wanted, and kept in the Air for at leaft five Minutes, when it will come to its proper Station, anfwerable to the Temperature of the Air.

The Refraction in Altitude taken out of the Table, p. 2. may, in like Manner as above, be corrected on account of the Barometer and Thermometer; but this will be of no great Confequence for correcting Altitudes taken from the Horizon of the Sea, as they can feldom be taken fo exact as the Di-ftance of the Moon from the Sun or Stars may; and the Exactnefs of a Minute is more than fefficient for all the Pur-pofes to which the Altitudes taken at Sea are at prefent ap-plied in the Practice of Navigation. But fhould an Obferver take Altitudes of the Sun or Stars at Land, for finding his Latitude or the Time of the Day, with a well-divided aftro-nomical Quadrant, or with a good Hadley's Quadrant, by the Help of Reflexion from a Bafon of Water or Quickfilver, defended from the Wind, in fuch Cafe it might be proper that he fhould firft correct the Refractions taken out of Table p. 2. in the Manner above explained, before he applies them to the Reduction of his Obfervations.

I cannot conclude this Subject without firft paying a Tribute of Juftice due to the Memories of thofe great Aftronomers, Dr. Halley and Dr. Bradley, in the following Remark; that as to the former, we owe the Hint of the Ufe that may be made of the Barometer and Thermometer in correcting aftro-nomical Refractions; fo to the latter we owe the firft Example of putting this Method in Practice, together with a more ac-curate Table of mean Refractions than was known before (fee p. 2.) and a moft excellent Rule expreffing the Changes of the fame Refractions, anfwering to the Variations of the Ther-mometer (the Subftance of which is given above) deduced from the Mean of a great many Obfervations, made with an Inftrument far fuperior to any before ufed in the Practice of Aftronomy.

A NEW

A NEW

METHOD

OF COMPUTING THE EFFECT OF

REFRACTION

AND

PARALLAX

UPON THE

MOON'S DISTANCE

FROM THE

SUN OR A FIXED STAR.

BY MR. DUNTHORNE.

A TABLE for reducing the apparent to the true Altitude
of the Moon. I.

Hor. Par.)	53.	54	55	56	57
Alt.)	Cor. +	Cor. +	Cor. +	Cor. +	Cor. +
o	′ ″	′ ″	′ ″	′ ″	′ ″
0	20. 0	21. 0	22. 0	23. 0	24. 0
1	28.31	29.31	30.31	31.31	32.31
2	34.23	35.23	36.23	37.23	38.23
3	38.20	39.20	40.20	41.20	42.20
4	41. 1	42. 1	43. 1	44. 1	45. 1
5	42.54	43.53	44.53	45.53	46.53
6	44.15	45.14	46.14	47.14	48.13
7	45.16	45.15	47.15	48.14	49.14
8	46. 0	46.59	47.58	48.58	49.57
9	46.32	47.32	48.31	49.30	50.29
10	46.57	47.56	48.55	49.54	50.53
11	47.15	48.14	49.13	50.12	51.11
12	47.27	48.26	49.25	50.23	51.22
13	47.35	48.34	49.32	50.31	51.29
14	47.40	48.38	49.36	50.35	51.33
15	47.42	48.40	49.38	50.36	51.34
16	47.40	48.38	49.35	50.33	51.31
17	47.36	48.34	49.31	50.29	51.26
18	47.31	48.29	49.25	50.22	51.19
19	47.23	48.20	49.16	50.13	51.10
20	47.13	48. 9	49. 6	50. 2	50.59
21	47. 2	47.58	48.54	49.50	50.46
22	46.48	47.44	48.39	49.35	50.31
23	46.33	47.29	48.24	49.19	50.14
24	46.18	47.12	48. 7	49. 2	49.57
25	46. 0	46.55	47.49	48.44	49.38
26	45.42	46.36	47.30	48.24	49.18
27	45.22	46.16	47. 9	48. 3	48.56
28	45. 1	45.54	46.47	47.40	48.33
29	44.39	45.31	46.24	47.16	48. 9
30	44.15	45. 7	45.59	46.51	47.43

A TABLE for reducing the apparent to the true Altitude
of the Moon. I. continued.

Hor. Par. ☽	58	59	60	61	62
Alt. ☽	Corⁿ. +	Corⁿ. +	Corⁿ. +	Corⁿ. +	Corⁿ. +
°	′ ″	′ ″	′ ″	′ ″	′ ″
0	25. 0	26. 0	27. 0	28. 0	29. 0
1	33. 31	34. 31	35. 31	36. 31	37. 31
2	39. 23	40. 23	41. 23	42. 23	43. 23
3	43. 20	44. 20	45. 19	46. 19	47. 19
4	46. 0	47. 0	48. 0	49. 0	50. 0
5	47. 52	48. 52	49. 52	50. 52	51. 52
6	49. 13	50. 13	51. 12	52. 12	53. 12
7	50. 14	51. 13	52. 13	53. 12	54. 12
8	50. 57	51. 56	52. 56	53. 55	54. 54
9	51. 29	52. 28	53. 27	54. 26	55. 26
10	51. 52	52. 51	53. 50	54. 50	55. 49
11	52. 9	53. 8	54. 7	55. 6	56. 5
12	52. 21	53. 19	54. 18	55. 17	56. 16
13	52. 29	53. 26	54. 25	55. 23	56. 22
14	52. 31	53. 29	54. 28	55. 26	56. 24
15	52. 31	53. 29	54. 27	55. 25	56. 23
16	52. 28	53. 26	54. 24	55. 21	56. 19
17	52. 23	53. 21	54. 18	55. 16	56. 13
18	52. 16	53. 13	54. 10	55. 7	56. 4
19	52. 6	53. 3	54. 0	54. 57	55. 53
20	51. 55	52. 51	53. 48	54. 44	55. 40
21	51. 41	52. 38	53. 34	54. 30	55. 26
22	51. 26	52. 22	53. 18	54. 13	55. 9
23	51. 10	52. 5	53. 0	53. 55	54. 51
24	50. 52	51. 47	52. 41	53. 36	54. 31
25	50. 32	51. 27	52. 21	53. 15	54. 10
26	50. 12	51. 5	51. 59	52. 53	53. 47
27	49. 49	50. 43	51. 36	52. 30	53. 23
28	49. 26	50. 19	51. 12	52. 5	52. 58
29	49. 1	49. 54	50. 46	51. 39	52. 31
30	48. 35	49. 27	50. 19	51. 11	52. 3

A TABLE for reducing the apparent to the true Altitude of the Moon. I. continued.

Hor. Par. D	53	54	55	56	57
Alt. D	Cor. +	Cor. +	Cor. +	Cor. +	Cor. +
°	′ ″	′ ″	′ ″	′ ″	′ ″
30	44. 15	45. 7	45. 59	46. 51	47. 43
31	43. 51	44. 43	45. 34	46. 25	47. 17
32	43. 26	44. 16	45. 7	45. 58	46. 49
33	42. 59	43. 50	44. 40	45. 30	46. 21
34	42. 32	43. 22	44. 11	45. 1	45. 51
35	42. 3	42. 53	43. 42	44. 31	45. 20
36	41. 34	42. 23	43. 12	44. 0	44. 48
37	41. 4	41. 52	42. 40	43. 28	44. 16
38	40. 33	41. 20	42. 7	42. 55	43. 42
39	40. 1	40. 47	41. 34	42. 21	43. 7
40	39. 28	40. 14	41. 0	41. 46	42. 32
41	38. 54	39. 40	40. 25	41. 10	41. 56
42	38. 20	39. 4	39. 49	40. 34	41. 18
43	37. 44	38. 29	39. 12	39. 56	40. 40
44	37. 8	37. 52	38. 35	39. 18	40. 1
45	36. 32	37. 14	37. 56	38. 39	39. 21
46	35. 54	36. 35	37. 17	37. 59	38. 41
47	35. 16	35. 56	36. 37	37. 18	37. 59
48	34. 37	35. 17	35. 57	36. 37	37. 17
49	33. 57	34. 36	35. 16	35. 55	36. 34
50	33. 16	33. 55	34. 34	35. 12	35. 51
51	32. 35	33. 13	33. 51	34. 29	35. 6
52	31. 54	32. 30	33. 7	33. 44	34. 21
53	31. 11	31. 47	32. 23	32. 59	33. 36
54	30. 28	31. 3	31. 39	32. 14	32. 49
55	29. 44	30. 19	30. 53	31. 28	32. 2
56	29. 0	29. 33	30. 7	30. 41	31. 14
57	28. 15	28. 48	29. 20	29. 53	30. 26
58	27. 30	28. 1	28. 33	29. 5	29. 37
59	26. 44	27. 14	27. 45	28. 16	28. 47
60	25. 57	26. 27	26. 57	27. 27	27. 57

A TABLE for reducing the apparent to the true Altitude of the Moon. I. continued.

Hor. Par. ☽	58	59	60	61	62
Alt. ☽	Corⁿ. +	Corⁿ. +	Corⁿ. +	Corⁿ. +	Corⁿ. +
○	′ ″	′ ″	′ ″	′ ″	′ ″
30	48.35	49.27	50.19	51.11	52. 3
31	48. 8	49. 0	49.51	50.43	51.34
32	47.40	48.31	49.22	50.13	51. 4
33	47.11	48. 1	48.52	49.42	50.32
34	46.41	47.30	48.20	49.10	50. 0
35	46. 9	46.58	47.47	48.37	49.26
36	45.37	46.25	47.14	48. 2	48.51
37	45. 3	45.51	46.39	47.27	48.15
38	44.29	45.16	46. 4	46.51	47.39
39	43.54	44.41	45.27	46.14	47. 1
40	43.18	44. 4	44.50	45.36	46.22
41	42.41	43.26	44.11	44.57	45.42
42	42. 3	42.47	43.32	44.17	45. 1
43	41.24	42. 8	42.52	43.36	44.19
44	40.44	41.27	42.11	42.54	43.37
45	40. 4	40.46	41.29	42.11	42.53
46	39.22	40. 4	40.46	41.27	42. 9
47	38.40	39.21	40. 2	40.43	41.24
48	37.57	38.37	39.18	39.58	40.38
49	37.14	37.53	38.32	39.12	39.51
50	36.29	37. 8	37.46	38.25	39. 3
51	35.44	36.22	37. 0	37.37	38.15
52	34.59	35.35	36.12	36.49	37.26
53	34.12	34.48	35.24	36. 0	36.36
54	33.24	34. 0	34.35	35.10	35.45
55	32.36	33.11	33.45	34.20	34.54
56	31.48	32.21	32.55	33.28	34. 2
57	30.58	31.31	32. 4	32.36	33. 9
58	30. 9	30.40	31.12	31.44	32.16
59	29.18	29.49	30.20	30.51	31.22
60	28.27	28.57	29.27	29.57	30.27

A TABLE for reducing the apparent to the true Altitude of the Moon. I. continued.

Hor. Par. ☽	53	54	55	56	57
Alt. ☽	Cor⁰. +	Cor⁰. +	Cor⁰. +	Cor⁰. +	Cor⁰. +
°	′ ″	′ ″	′ ″	′ ″	′ ″
60	25. 57	26. 27	25. 57	27. 27	27. 57
61	25. 10	25. 39	26. 8	26. 37	27. 6
62	24. 22	24. 51	25. 19	25. 47	26. 15
63	23. 35	24. 2	24. 29	24. 56	25. 23
64	22. 46	23. 12	23. 39	24. 5	24. 31
65	21. 57	22. 23	22. 48	23. 13	23. 39
66	21. 9	21. 32	21. 57	22. 21	22. 46
67	20. 18	20. 42	21. 5	21. 29	21. 52
68	19. 28	19. 51	20. 13	20. 36	20. 58
69	18. 38	18. 59	19. 21	19. 42	20. 4
70	17. 47	18. 7	18. 28	18. 49	19. 9
71	16. 56	17. 15	17. 35	17. 54	18. 14
72	16. 4	16. 23	16. 41	17. 0	17. 18
73	15. 12	15. 30	15. 47	16. 5	16. 23
74	14. 20	14. 37	14. 53	15. 10	15. 26
75	13. 28	13. 43	13. 59	14. 14	14. 30
76	12. 35	12. 50	13. 4	13. 19	13. 33
77	11. 42	11. 56	12. 9	12. 23	12. 36
78	10. 49	11. 2	11. 14	11. 27	11. 39
79	9. 55	10. 7	10. 19	10. 30	10. 42
80	9. 2	9. 13	9. 23	9. 33	9. 44
81	8. 8	8. 18	8. 27	8. 37	8. 46
82	7. 15	7. 23	7. 31	7. 40	7. 48
83	6. 21	6. 28	6. 35	6. 42	6. 50
84	5. 26	5. 33	5. 39	5. 45	5. 51
85	4. 32	4. 37	4. 43	4. 48	4. 53
86	3. 38	3. 42	3. 46	3. 50	3. 55
87	2. 43	2. 47	2. 50	2. 53	2. 56
88	1. 49	1. 51	1. 53	1. 55	1. 57
89	0. 54	0. 56	0. 57	0. 58	0. 59
90	0. 0	0. 0	0. 0	0. 0	0. 0

A TABLE for reducing the apparent to the true Altitude of the Moon. I. concluded.

Hor. Par. ☽	′ 58	′ 59	′ 60	′ 61	′ 62
Alt. ☽	Cor⁰. +	Cor⁰. +	Cor⁰. +	Cor⁰. +	Cor⁰. +
°	′ ″	′ ″	′ ″	′ ″	′ ″
60	28. 27	28. 57	29. 27	29. 57	30. 27
61	27. 35	28. 4	28. 34	29. 3	29. 32
62	26. 43	27. 11	27. 40	28. 8	28. 36
63	25. 51	26. 18	26. 45	27. 12	27. 40
64	24. 58	25. 24	25. 50	26. 17	26. 43
65	24. 4	24. 30	24. 55	25. 20	25. 46
66	23. 10	23. 34	23. 59	24. 23	24. 48
67	22. 16	22. 39	23. 2	23. 26	23. 49
68	21. 21	21. 43	22. 6	22. 28	22. 51
69	20. 25	20. 47	21. 8	21. 30	21. 51
70	19. 30	19. 50	20. 11	20. 31	20. 52
71	18. 33	18. 53	19. 12	19. 32	19. 52
72	17. 37	17. 55	18. 14	18. 33	18. 51
73	16. 40	16. 58	17. 15	17. 33	17. 50
74	15. 43	16. 0	16. 16	16. 33	16. 49
75	14. 46	15. 1	15. 17	15. 32	15. 48
76	13. 48	14. 2	14. 17	14. 31	14. 46
77	12. 50	13. 3	13. 17	13. 30	13. 44
78	11. 51	12. 4	12. 16	12. 29	12. 41
79	10. 53	11. 4	11. 16	11. 27	11. 39
80	9. 54	10. 5	10. 15	10. 25	10. 36
81	8. 55	9. 5	9. 14	9. 24	9. 33
82	7. 56	8. 5	8. 13	8. 21	8. 30
83	6. 57	7. 4	7. 12	7. 19	7. 26
84	5. 58	6. 4	6. 10	6. 17	6. 23
85	4. 58	5. 4	5. 9	5. 14	5. 19
86	3. 59	4. 3	4. 7	4. 11	4. 15
87	2. 59	3. 3	3. 5	3. 9	3. 12
88	1. 59	2. 2	2. 4	2. 6	2. 8
89	1. 0	1. 1	1. 2	1. 3	1. 4
90	0. 0	0. 0	0. 0	0. 0	0. 0

H

o

A TABLE of Logarithmic Differences for readily computing the true Distance of the Moon from a Fixed Star.
II.

Hor. Par. D	53	54	55	56	57
Alt D	Log. Diff.	Log. Diff.	Log. Diff.	Log. Diff.	Log. Diff.
0					
0	+ 11.3	+ 11.2	+ 11.1	+ 11.0	+ 10.9
1	+ 4.2	+ 3.9	+ 3.6	+ 3.2	+ 2.9
2	− 5.3	− 5.9	− 6.5	− 7.1	− 7.6
3	16.1	16.9	17.7	18.5	19.3
4	27.3	28.4	29.4	30.5	31.5
5	38.8	40.1	41.3	42.6	43.9
6	50.4	51.9	53.4	54.9	56.3
7	62.0	63.7	65.5	67.2	68.9
8	73.6	75.6	77.5	79.4	81.4
9	85.2	87.4	89.5	91.7	93.8
10	96.8	99.1	101.5	103.9	106.3
11	108.3	110.9	113.5	116.1	118.7
12	119.7	122.6	125.4	128.2	131.0
13	131.2	134.2	137.2	140.3	143.3
14	142.6	145.8	149.0	152.3	155.6
15	154.0	157.4	160.9	164.3	167.8
16	165.2	168.9	172.5	176.2	179.9
17	176.4	180.3	184.2	188.1	192.0
18	187.6	191.7	195.8	199.9	204.0
19	198.7	203.1	207.3	211.6	216.0
20	209.8	214.2	218.8	223.3	227.8
21	220.8	225.5	230.2	234.9	239.6
22	231.6	236.5	241.4	246.3	251.3
23	242.3	247.5	252.6	257.8	262.9
24	253.2	258.4	263.8	269.1	274.5
25	263.7	269.3	274.8	280.4	285.9
26	274.3	280.1	285.9	291.6	297.3
27	284.8	290.8	296.7	302.7	308.5
28	295.2	301.3	307.4	313.6	319.7
29	303.5	311.7	318.1	324.4	330.8
30	315.6	322.1	328.7	335.2	341.7

A TABLE of Logarithmic Differences for readily computing the true Distance of the Moon from a Fixed Star. II. continued.

Hor. Par. ⟩	58	59	60	61	62
Alt ⟩	Log. Diff.	Log. Diff.	Log. Diff.	Log. Diff.	Log. Diff.
0					
0	+ 10.8	+ 10.8	+ 10.7	+ 10.6	+ 10.4
1	+ 2.5	+ 2.2	+ 1.8	+ 1.5	+ 1.1
2	— 8.2	— 8.8	— 9.4	— 10.0	— 10.6
3	20.1	21.0	21.8	22.6	23.5
4	32.5	33.6	34.7	35.7	36.8
5	45.1	46.4	47.7	49.0	50.3
6	57.8	59.4	60.8	62.4	63.9
7	70.6	72.3	74.1	75.8	77.6
8	83.3	85.3	87.2	89.2	91.1
9	96.0	98.2	100.3	102.5	104.7
10	108.6	111.0	113.4	115.9	118.2
11	121.3	123.9	125.5	129.1	131.7
12	133.8	136.6	139.5	142.3	145.2
13	146.4	149.4	152.4	155.5	158.5
14	158.8	162.0	165.4	168.6	171.9
15	171.2	174.7	178.2	181.7	185.2
16	183.5	187.1	191.0	194.5	198.3
17	195.8	199.8	203.7	207.6	211.5
18	208.1	212.2	216.3	220.4	224.6
19	220.2	224.6	228.9	233.3	237.6
20	232.3	236.8	241.4	245.9	250.4
21	244.4	249.1	253.8	258.6	263.3
22	256.2	261.2	266.1	271.0	276.0
23	268.1	273.2	278.3	283.5	288.6
24	279.8	285.2	290.5	295.8	301.2
25	291.4	297.0	302.5	308.1	313.7
26	303.1	308.7	314.5	320.2	326.0
27	314.4	320.4	326.3	332.3	338.3
28	325.8	332.0	338.1	344.3	350.4
29	337.0	343.4	349.7	356.1	362.4
30	348.2	354.7	361.3	367.8	374.3

A TABLE of Logarithmic Differences for readily computing the true Distance of the Moon from a Fixed Star.
II. continued.

Hor. Par. ☽	53	54	55	56	57
Alt. ☽	Log. Diff.	Log. Diff.	Log. Diff.	Log. Diff.	Log. Diff.
°					
30	315.6	322.1	328.7	335.2	341.7
31	325.7	332.4	339.1	345.8	352.5
32	335.7	342.5	349.4	356.3	363.2
33	345.5	352.6	359.7	366.8	373.8
34	355.3	362.6	369.8	377.1	384.3
35	364.9	372.3	379.8	387.2	394.7
36	374.4	382.0	389.7	397.3	404.9
37	383.8	391.6	399.3	407.2	415.0
38	393.1	401.1	409.0	417.0	425.0
39	402.3	410.4	418.5	426.7	434.8
40	411.3	419.6	427.9	436.2	444.6
41	420.2	428.7	437.2	445.6	454.1
42	428.9	437.6	446.2	454.9	463.5
43	437.5	446.4	455.2	464.0	472.8
44	446.0	455.0	464.0	472.9	481.9
45	454.4	463.5	472.6	481.8	490.9
46	462.6	471.8	481.1	490.4	499.7
47	470.6	480.0	489.5	498.9	508.4
48	478.5	488.1	497.7	507.3	516.9
49	486.3	496.0	505.7	515.5	525.2
50	493.9	503.8	513.6	523.5	533.4
51	501.4	511.4	521.4	531.4	541.4
52	508.7	518.8	529.0	539.1	549.3
53	515.9	526.1	536.3	546.6	556.9
54	522.7	533.2	543.6	554.0	564.4
55	529.5	540.1	550.6	561.2	571.7
56	536.1	546.8	557.5	568.1	578.8
57	542.6	553.4	564.2	574.9	585.7
58	548.8	559.7	570.6	581.6	592.5
59	554.9	565.9	577.0	588.0	599.1
60	560.8	571.9	583.1	594.2	605.4

A TABLE of Logarithmic Differences for readily computing the true Distance of the Moon from a Fixed Star. II. continued.

Hor. Par. ☽	58	59	60	61	62
Alt. ☽	Log. Diff.	Log. Diff.	Log. Diff.	Log. Diff.	Log. Diff.
°					
30	348.2	354.7	361.3	367.8	374.3
31	359.2	366.0	372.7	379.4	386.1
32	370.1	377.1	383.9	390.9	397.8
33	380.9	388.0	395.1	402.2	409.3
34	391.6	398.9	406.1	413.4	420.7
35	402.1	409.6	417.0	424.5	432.0
36	412.5	420.2	427.8	435.5	443.1
37	422.9	430.6	438.5	446.3	454.1
38	433.0	441.6	449.0	457.0	465.0
39	443.0	451.2	459.3	467.5	475.7
40	452.9	461.2	469.5	477.9	486.2
41	462.7	471.1	479.6	488.1	496.7
42	472.2	480.9	489.5	498.2	506.9
43	481.6	490.5	499.3	508.1	517.0
44	490.9	499.9	508.9	517.9	526.9
45	500.0	509.2	518.3	527.5	536.6
46	509.0	518.3	527.6	536.9	546.2
47	517.8	527.3	536.7	546.2	555.6
48	526.5	536.1	545.7	555.3	564.9
49	535.0	544.7	554.5	564.2	574.0
50	543.3	553.2	563.1	573.0	582.9
51	551.4	561.5	571.5	581.5	591.6
52	559.4	569.6	579.8	589.9	600.1
53	567.2	577.6	587.8	598.1	608.5
54	574.8	585.3	595.7	606.1	616.6
55	582.3	592.8	603.4	614.0	624.5
56	589.5	600.2	610.9	621.6	632.3
57	596.6	607.4	618.2	629.0	639.8
58	603.4	614.3	625.2	636.2	647.1
59	610.1	621.1	632.1	643.2	654.2
60	616.5	627.7	638.8	650.0	661.2

A TABLE of Logarithmic Differences for readily computing the true Distance of the Moon from a Fixed Star.
II. continued.

Hor. Par. D	′ 53	′ 54	′ 55	′ 56	′ 57
Alt. D	Log. Diff.	Log. Diff.	Log. Diff.	Log. Diff.	Log. Diff.
°					
60	560.8	571.9	583.1	594.2	605.4
61	566.5	577.8	589.0	600.3	611.5
62	572.1	583.5	594.8	606.2	617.5
63	577.6	589.0	600.4	611.9	623.4
64	582.8	594.3	605.9	617.4	629.0
65	587.9	599.5	611.0	622.8	634.4
66	592.7	604.4	616.2	627.9	639.7
67	597.3	609.2	621.0	632.8	644.7
68	601.8	613.8	625.7	637.6	649.5
69	606.1	618.2	630.2	642.2	654.2
70	610.2	622.3	634.4	646.5	658.5
71	614.2	626.3	638.5	650.6	662.7
72	617.8	630.1	642.4	654.5	666.7
73	621.1	633.7	645.9	658.2	670.5
74	624.7	637.0	649.4	661.7	674.2
75	627.9	640.3	652.7	665.1	677.5
76	630.9	643.3	655.7	658.2	680.6
77	633.6	646.0	658.5	671.1	683.6
78	636.0	648.6	661.2	673.7	686.3
79	638.3	650.9	663.5	676.1	688.7
80	640.5	653.1	665.7	678.3	691.0
81	642.3	654.9	667.7	680.4	693.1
82	644.0	656.7	669.4	682.2	694.9
83	645.5	658.2	671.0	683.8	696.5
84	646.9	659.5	672.3	685.2	697.9
85	647.9	560.7	673.5	686.4	699.1
86	648.8	661.6	674.5	687.3	700.1
87	649.5	662.3	675.2	688.0	700.9
88	650.1	662.9	676.0	688.5	701.5
89	650.3	663.2	676.2	688.9	701.8

A TABLE of Logarithmic Differences for readily computing the true Distance of the Moon from a Fixed Star.
II. concluded.

Hor. Par. ☽	58	59	60	61	61
Alt. ☽	Log. Diff.	Log. Diff.	Log. Diff.	Log. Diff.	Log. Diff.
o					
60	616.5	627.7	638.8	650.0	661.2
61	622.8	634.0	645.3	656.6	667.9
62	628.9	640.3	651.6	663.0	674.4
63	634.8	646.3	657.8	669.2	680.7
64	640.6	652.1	663.7	675.3	686.9
65	646.1	657.8	669.4	681.1	692.8
66	651.4	663.2	674.9	686.7	698.4
67	656.5	668.3	680.2	692.0	703.9
68	661.4	673.3	685.3	697.2	709.2
69	666.2	678.1	690.2	702.2	714.2
70	670.6	682.7	694.8	706.9	719.0
71	674.9	687.0	699.2	711.3	723.5
72	678.9	691.2	703.4	715.6	727.9
73	682.8	695.1	707.4	719.7	732.0
74	686.5	698.8	711.2	723.5	735.9
75	689.9	702.3	714.7	727.1	739.6
76	693.2	705.6	718.1	730.6	743.0
77	696.1	708.5	721.2	733.8	746.2
78	698.8	711.4	724.0	736.6	749.1
79	701.3	714.0	726.5	739.2	751.8
80	703.6	716.3	729.0	741.6	754.3
81	705.7	718.4	731.1	743.8	756.5
82	707.6	720.3	733.1	745.8	758.5
83	709.3	722.0	734.8	747.5	760.3
84	710.7	723.5	736.2	748.9	761.8
85	711.9	724.7	737.5	750.1	763.1
86	712.9	725.7	738.5	751.3	764.2
87	713.7	726.5	739.3	752.1	765.0
88	714.2	727.1	740.0	752.8	765.6
89	714.5	727.3	740.3	753.1	766.0

U · S · E

T A B L E S.

Problem.

HAVING the apparent or obferved Diftance of the
Moon from a Fixed Star, together with the obferved
Altitude of each, to find their true Diftance.

Solution.

With the Moon's horizontal Parallax, and apparent Altitude, take out the Correction of her Altitude from Table I.
alfo the logarithmic Difference from Table II. which referve;
and to the Correction of the Moon's Altitude add the Refraction of the Star; this Sum added to or fubftracted from
the Difference of the obferved Altitudes, according as the
Moon is higher or lower than the Star, gives the Difference
of their true Altitudes.

Then, from the Natural-cofine of the Difference of the apparent Altitudes fubftract the Natural-cofine of the obferved
Diftance, and find the Logarithm of the Remainder; from
which take the logarithmic Difference before referved, and
you will have a Logarithm, whofe correfponding Number
fubftracted from the Natural-cofine of the Difference of their
true Altitudes leaves the Natural-cofine of the true Diftance
required.

Example.

[65]

EXAMPLE.

(From Mr. MASKELYNE's Mariner's Guide, p. 17, &c.)

1762, May 9, at 12ʰ. 34′. 19″ apparent Time at Greenwich, according to Account at Sea,

	° ′ ″
The apparent Distance of the Moon's Centre from Spica Virginis was . . . . }	51. 28. 35

The apparent Altitude of the Star	24. 48
The apparent Altitude of the Moon's Centre . .	12. 30

Difference of the apparent or observed Altitudes	12. 18

	′ ″	
Correction of the Moon's Altitude from Table I. . . . . }	50. 42	}
Refraction of the Star	2. 3	}
Sum subtracted		52. 45

Difference of their true Altitudes	11. 25. 15

Natural-cosine of the Difference of apparent Altitudes . . . . }	97705
Natural-cosine of 51°. 28′. 35″, the apparent Distance . . . . }	62283

Difference of the Natural-cosines	35422

Logarithm thereof	4·54927
Logarithmic Difference taken from Table II. subtract . . . . }	135

Remainder	4·54792

Number corresponding thereunto	35312

Natural-cosine of 11°. 25′. 15″, the Difference of their true Altitudes . . . . }	98920
From which subtract the above corresponding Number . . . . }	35312

Leaves Natural-cosine of 51°. 9′. 54″, the Moon's true Distance from the Star . . . . . }	62708

I   Note.

Note: If only the firft five Figures of the Sines and Logarithms be ufed, they will commonly determine the Moon's true Diftance from a Star, within 5'', or at moft 10''; in which Cafe, the laft figures of the logarithmic Differences is to be omitted, and if the Star's Altitude be above 5°, the remaining Figures will need no Correction: but if greater Exactnefs be defired, fo that fix Figures of the Sines and Logarithms be taken, all the Figures in the Table of logarithmic Differences are to be made ufe of; and if the Star's Altitude does not exceed 25°, are to be increafed, as in the following Table.

Alt. of the Star.	Particles to be added to Log. Diff.	Alt. of the Star.	Particles to be added to Log. Diff.
o		o	
2	4.4	10	0.4
3	2.7	11	0.3
4	1.8	12	0.3
5	1.3	13	0.2
6	0.9	14	0.2
7	0.7	15	0.1
8	0.6	20	0.1
9	0.5	25	0.1

Invefligation of the foregoing Solution.

In the fpherical Triangle B A C, wherein A reprefents the Zenith, B the Moon, and C the Star, are given the three Sides, to find how much the Bafe BC is altered, by varying the Sides AB and AC, while the Angle at the Vertex A remains the fame.

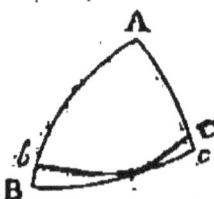

As Sine AB x Sine AC : R? :: Ver.-fine BC — Ver.-fine $\overline{AB — AC}$: Ver.-fine A.

And. as Sine A b x Sine A c : R? :: Ver.-fine bc — Ver.-fine $— \overline{Ab — Ac}$: Ver.-fine A. Per Cafwell Trigon. Axiom. 4.

Then